RUNNING WITH
THE TIGER

ANSIE LEE SPERRY

RUNNING WITH THE TIGER

A Memoir of an Extraordinary Young Woman's Life
in Hong Kong, China, the South Pacific
and POW Camp

ansieleesperrymemoirs@gmail.com

ISBN: 1442112506

To my late husband, Henry.
I am grateful for his steadfast belief in me and
whatever I chose to do. A lot of good things
came out of my years in internment camp, and
the best thing was meeting Henry.

TABLE OF CONTENTS

MAPS

PREFACE

My mother, Ansie Lee Sperry, was born in 1914, the year of the Tiger, one of the twelve animals in the Chinese Zodiac. Tigers are considered to be: adventurous, idealistic, competitive, unpredictable, able to overcome obstacles with confidence, creative, full of social grace and charismatic.

I find it uncanny how these Tiger characteristics perfectly describe my mother. What an adventurer she was, as well as an idealist who wanted to "do her bit" for her country. She left her family and a comfortable life in Hong Kong in 1939 to volunteer for the Chinese Red Cross in the interior of a China that was already at war. Her pluck while interned as a civilian POW in the Philippines during World War II allowed her to overcome the many obstacles she encountered. Her creativity extends from her art to her approach to life. At age ninety-four, she is a vibrant woman with a contagious enthusiasm that draws people to her.

The Tiger is said to be compatible with the Horse, and my late father, Henry M. Sperry, was born in 1906, the year of the Horse. Ansie and Henry met in internment camp (my father always said they met "in jail") and married in Shanghai after the war in 1946. Henry supported Ansie unconditionally in whatever adventures she cooked up during the fifty-seven years they were married, until his death in 2003 at the age of 96.

I always knew my mother had led an exciting life, but when I first read this memoir I was thrilled at how beautifully she writes and how her diary, her sketches and photographs make her story come alive. I hope you will find it as enjoyable to read as I did.

Victoria Sperry Merchant

ACKNOWLEDGMENTS

My fourth brother, the late Jung Sen (known as J.S.) Lee, was very helpful in giving me details of our family history. We were not only brother and sister, we were great friends as well. J.S.'s son Chien Lee provided me with family photos.

Frank Bren in Australia has been collecting material to write a book on W. H. Donald's life and provided me with copies of many documents relating to Donald.

Mary Hossfeld provided editorial assistance, Sue Oksanen helped the process along and Phyllis Browning provided computer assistance. Karen Minot Illustration created the map graphics. Hayoung Heidi Lee took the author photograph on my 94th birthday. My daughter Vicky Merchant helped pull the book together.

To all of them, I give my heartfelt thanks. I enjoyed every minute of writing this memoir.

Ansie Lee Sperry
Portola Valley, California
May 2009

AUTHOR'S NOTES

While the book is written with American usage, the excerpts from my diaries retain the original British usage, reflecting my education in British schools. I have occasionally rephrased some of my diary passages.

The photographs are from my personal collection or from the collection of my late brother J.S. Lee. In Chapter 9, the photograph of W. H. Donald and Generalissimo and Madame Chiang Kai-Shek was given to me by Donald. The source of this photograph is unknown, although every attempt has been made to locate the photographer and original copyright owner.

The place names indicated in the maps are the historical names that were in use at the time of my travels.

RUNNING WITH THE TIGER

CHAPTER 1
FAIRY TALE

Long, long ago, in the misty past, a farmer looked over his field of golden grain and summoned his family to gather their reaping hooks to start harvesting. It was this scene that became the pictograph of the character Li 利 , which was chosen as a family surname. This is our name, anglicized by Grandfather into "Lee." My brother J.S. told me that in the whole of Hong Kong with its millions of Chinese there are but a handful with this surname and they all come from the small area of Sze Yup, with four villages. Our family is from the village of Sun Wui. All around it are streams and waterways, this being the delta of the Chu (Pearl) River flowing into the South China Sea.

We were not always southerners. At home during my childhood, fragrant flowers and fruits were placed at the altar for Buddha and other gods and next to that was a large red tablet dedicated to our ancestors from Honan. On the first and fifteenth days of the lunar calendar as well as festival days, Chieh, my Mother, would gather us into the prayer room to bow at the two altars. Looking up and reading "Honan" on the large red tablet, we would offer burning incense sticks, trying not to sneeze from the wisps of smoke. Honan is not a southern province, but far to the north and center of China.

In January of 1971, a site for a hospital was being dug near Changsha, Hunan Province. It was not long before the workers found they were breaking into the top of a tomb. The work was abandoned and excavations were taken over by archaeologists.

The workers had struck white clay, a 54-inch layer of which solidly surrounded a 15 - 20-inch layer of charcoal, which encased a wooden tomb chamber. The depth of the pit was 22 yards at the bottom, creating a perfectly insulated crypt.

Buried inside was a woman who was the wife of the first Marquis of Tai, who governed in 163-186 BC. The Marquis's name was Li-Ts'ang, the "Li" being the same character as ours.

The Marquis must have loved his wife greatly as he lavished her with the finest of worldly goods. Lady Li was shrouded in twenty layers of beautiful garments and embroidered coverlets. She did not have one coffin, but was encased in four, fitted one inside the other. Attending her were 200 wooden figures, some dressed in silk as attendants, and some as dancers. Two entirely new types of musical instruments were found, as well as a new method of applying polychrome paintings on silk. There were 300 pieces of tomb furniture and 184 objects made of lacquer, their sheen lustrous as new. As for her two vanity cases, experts claimed they were the finest ever seen from the Han dynasty.

However, all the trappings were nothing compared to the lady herself. After 2,000 years the body had escaped decay, the skin and muscles were still pliable, and the internal organs appeared intact. This discovery was widely hailed as a miracle in medical history and archaeology.

Lady Li's blood type was group A. One hundred thirty-eight muskmelon seeds were found in her internal organs; she had died soon after eating the melon. She was 5'1" tall and about fifty years old.

Our venerable "Aunt" with her worldly goods can be viewed at the Hunan Provincial Museum in Changsha, China.

CHAPTER 2
FATHER

In 1935 a package arrived for our family in Hong Kong from Penang, a small British resort on the western coast of Malaysia. It contained documents recording the name, date and time of birth of each male infant of our Lee family over a period of 700 years. The sender was Lee Hin Shang, a total stranger.

The Lee family moved from Central China and settled in Hoiping in the Sze Yup district on the southern coast of China in Kwangtung Province. Our Grandfather Lee Leung Yik, was born in that district in 1841. Grandfather, along with his brother Man Yik, followed the example of many of the villagers of that area. They had married and produced male heirs, and were free to sail across the Pacific to seek their fortune in North America. "Gold Mountain," they called California, after the discovery of gold in 1849. However, the two brothers did not labor at the mines, but worked at the Union Cigar Company at 17 Dupont Street in San Francisco.

Father was born on the twentieth day of the ninth moon in 1880. He was the eighteenth generation to be inscribed in the Lee records. When Father was eleven years old, his father sent for him to join him in America. So the young lad, accompanied by a cousin, crossed the Pacific Ocean to California, passing through immigration on Angel Island in San Francisco Bay. They studied at the Chinese Primary School on Clay Street in San Francisco.

A few years later, in 1896, the two brothers decided they had saved enough money and left California, taking the two boys with them. Not one of them returned to America. When Grandfather came back to China, he moved the family to Sun Wui, a neighboring village and a place safer from bandits. One great aunt had already been kidnapped for ransom. The bandits took out all her gold teeth. When she returned home, undaunted, she had silver ones made.

Grandfather and his brother left the village the next year and started a business in Hong Kong, a British Colony. They imported blue cloth from China and exported it to Malaya. This was in 1897, the year Hong Kong celebrated Queen Victoria's Diamond Jubilee. Father enrolled at Queen's College as student No. 6,707, under the name of Li Shin.[1] To have an English education at Queen's College, the Eton or Harrow of the Colony, was part of the key to Father's success.

The following year, 1898, a marriage was arranged for the 18-year-old student Li Shin, and he returned to the village to wed Wong Lan-Fong.

The bride was carefully chosen for him by his parents through a go-between, a woman whose job was to be in contact with other

---

[1] The information about Father while in Queen's College is from the book, *Queen's College 1862-1962*, by Gwenneth Stokes. (Hong Kong, Queen's College, 1962.)

families in order to match up suitable spouses for the teenagers. The bride-to-be, Miss Wong, came from Toi Shan, a neighboring county and had tiny feet. Being gentry, she did not have to toil in the fields. From babyhood her parents had bound her feet so that they could not grow properly. Gradually and painfully, the toes were curled down to touch the pads of her feet and the arches humped up. To walk she had to take small steps and to keep her balance she would shift her hips so it created a wiggle which was considered alluring. The bride was pretty, with an engaging smile and a regal bearing. Father was devoted to her throughout his life.

Father continued his English studies at Queen's College. When he graduated he was asked to be a "Pupil Teacher," a most grueling task of long hours of study and teaching the Lower Forms. There were some sixty boys in his class. He taught in the main hall, where two other classes were in session. There were no partitions or platforms, and no large ceiling fans to stir up the air in the damp heat of the long Hong Kong summers.

As was the custom, Father changed his name as he grew to manhood. When he was a little tot, the family fondly called him by some droll name (to deceive the evil one from snatching him away). Later he was called Ting Sien. When he started out in the business world, he chose Hysan as his name. (Hysan is pronounced Hay Sun in Cantonese and High San in English.)

Father was socially engaging. At reunions of the Queen's College Old Boys' Association, there was mention of "the lavish supply of champagne." This he provided for the school's dinners. There were references to Father's generous gifts to the school, among them were three scholarships: the Lee Hysan; the Grant, in honor of a school Master; and the third in memory of his old friend, Kong Ki Fai. He gave generously to promote education, especially to the University of Hong Kong and St. Paul's Girls' School.

Father grew tall and handsome, with high cheekbones and a ruddy complexion. He always wore Chinese clothes: long gowns, cloth shoes and black bindings around the edges of his trousers. Although his peers sported suits and ties, Father, with his regal bearing, stood apart looking every inch a merchant prince.

Father

Father was successful in business from the start. At 21 he became manager of a firm in Hong Kong called Sui Wing Chang that imported Chinese medicines and dried foods from China and exported them to South East Asia. His knowledge of English in a British Colony and his personality and brains made an unbeatable combination. Father's second position was with a shipping company owned by the Singapore Chinese Trading Co. He broadened his knowledge of the world by taking trips to Singapore, Malaya and Rangoon. He soon had his own shipping company, but World War I interrupted that venture.

Father took over the property at 202 Queens Road Central from his father and uncle. Here their firm Lai Cheung Loong carried on the import-export of blue cloth from China. He registered his new company at this address, and he named it Lee Hysan Co. In 1923 he changed it to Lee Hysan Estate Co., Ltd. Father and his wife lived nearby on Gow Yee Fong where they could see the waterfront and knew when his company's ship sailed in.

In 1904, after six years of marriage with one baby daughter who did not survive, Father brought home a concubine. She was 18 years old, petite, very bright and a city girl born in Canton. Her name was Cheung Shui Leen.

The first wife, Wong Lan Fong, was not sure how tall this new addition to the household would be, so she stood on a little footstool to be sure she would look down on the new concubine as she crossed the threshold. She need not have worried. Cheung Shui Leen was small and slim. This little concubine went on her knees to kowtow[2] to "Nai-Nai," and offered her a cup of tea to show

---

[2]Kowtow: to kneel and touch the forehead to the ground in token of homage, worship or deep respect. In *Merriam-Webster Online Dictionary*. Retrieved January 27, 2009, from http://www.merriam-webster.com/dictionary/kowtow

signs of obedience. From that moment she became a member of the family. Chieh, as we all called her, soon fit into the household as she was in fact very docile, very religious and smart enough to know her place.

Chieh became pregnant and Father was overjoyed and hired an English midwife to be sure things would go smoothly. On March 7, 1905, his first son was born. Ming Chak was later known as Richard Charles Lee, "Dick" to his friends and "Elder Brother" to his brothers and sisters.

The first wife, whom we children called Ah Ma, soon after started her family of two sons and two daughters. (According to Chinese custom, a wife was always called Ah Ma (Mother) by all the children, even those born to their father's concubines.)

My mother Chieh bore five children altogether, two sons and three daughters. Father took two more concubines, So Suk Han and Ng Pui Shan. My mother was known as Yee Chieh (*yee* meaning second) and the others were Sam Chieh (third) and Say Chieh (fourth). In all, the four wives bore Father fifteen children, seven boys and eight girls.[3] The oldest girl, who died at birth, was still counted as the first girl, so my youngest sister is called "Eighth Sister."

Because of periodic outbreaks of plague in Hong Kong, Father moved the family to Macao, and he commuted between the Portuguese and British colonies. When his sons were older they went to school in Hong Kong, and later Dick and another brother Harold went to Oxford University in England.

In 1913 Father was elected a Director of the Tung Wah Hospitals. These hospitals are solely for the poor and, to this day, these honorary posts are given to citizens who have achieved the

---

[3] See Appendix I for the Lee Family Tree

respect of the Colony for outstanding contributions to the community.

Father was keenly interested in the youngsters of Hong Kong and was responsible for the grant of a large piece of Hong Kong government land in Caroline Hill to be used by the public for athletics. He became the first President of the South China Athletic Association. His contribution to the expansion of the St. Paul's Girls' School was second only to that of the Hong Kong Government.

In 1925 Father purchased Jardine Hill in Causeway Bay from Jardine Matheson & Co. There were two mansions on the hill for the two top executives, the Taipan and the Yeepan of the company. There were stables and well-kept grounds. This purchase prompted the Governor, Sir Reginald Stubbs, to write a letter to Father congratulating him on the colony's biggest sale of land to a private individual. The family never lived at the Taipan houses but used the main one for entertaining and for the wedding receptions of my eldest brother Dick to Esther Wong in 1928 and for sister Doris to Kenneth Cheang in 1937.

At the bottom of Jardine Hill Father made an amusement park with games of chance and skill: coconut shies (tossing games), shooting galleries and, of course, several eating stalls and a large restaurant. He named it Lee Gardens. Colored lights and blaring music in the cool of the evening attracted throngs that spilled out of the trams from the western and central districts.

The following year, Father erected the Lee Theatre, an imposing building for Chinese Opera near Lee Gardens on Percival Street, Causeway Bay. It had a revolving stage, a marvel of the times. As a youngster, looking up at the dome inside the theatre, I was entranced by the sight of the heavens completely filled with dragons weaving in and out of clouds and lit by a burst of light from the center. Framing the stage were two columns, sculpted as clouds and hollowed out so one could see dragons inside, glowing in a warm orange light. Around the upstairs balcony were painted panels of historical scenes.

Lee Theatre

For years, whenever entertainers in need of a large stage visited our art-starved Colony, the Lee Theatre would be chosen as the venue for ballets, musicals, acrobats, famous singers, and local benefits. Later, when the popularity of Chinese opera waned, we used it mainly as a movie theatre. Other properties that Father owned were apartment buildings on Leighton Hill Road and Lee Tung Street in Wanchai.

Father believed strongly in education. He was exceptional in that he regarded his daughters to be as worthy of opportunities for learning as his sons. Before he died, he sent four of his children to England: Dick, Harold, sister Doris and me.

About the time of the First World War, Father joined Yu Hing Co. with Ma Chi Loong and Ma Jui Chiu. This import firm was one of many that put in a bid for a license from the Hong Kong government to import opium. In those years trading and using opium was legal, and many of our friends were involved.

On April 30, 1928, Father went off as usual into town to his office at Lai Cheung Loong on Queens Road, and then probably visited friends and discussed business with various banks. He might have visited the Hong Kong Shanghai Bank about the loan for his purchase of the Jardine property. Or he might have seen the Compradore of The National City Bank (now Citibank), Yiu Gueh Yuan. He was Father's Queen's College schoolmate and the bank's Chinese manager who was responsible for all Chinese matters as well as the local staff.

Lunch hour for businessmen in the Colony was 1 p.m. Father went as usual to the Yue Kee Club on Wellington Street. It was inside a passageway near the entrance that a man fired three bullets, hitting Father's shoulder and stomach and the back of Father's neck when he turned. His assassin escaped in the crowds of downtown Victoria. Family and friends were not aware that Father had any enemies, although recently he had won a court case in Macao concerning distribution of opium. The police could not shed any light on the matter.

When Father died, he left his wife and three concubines, seven sons and seven daughters (including the youngest daughter who was born later that year) to mourn him. Four of his children were away in England. He was only forty-seven years old. The family followed the burial rites of a Buddhist funeral. His many friends and associates bowed to his portrait in the Farewell Pavilion at the western end of the city.

The family mournfully laid Father to rest high up on the side of a hill with a view of islands and the vast shimmering sea meeting the sky.

CHAPTER 3
MACAO, MY BIRTHPLACE

Macao was a Portuguese colony founded in 1557, almost three hundred years before the Chinese ceded Hong Kong to Britain. The town itself was built on a peninsula, about two square miles with a gentle hill to the east. It is joined to the vast continent of Asia by a narrow isthmus into South China. My family had moved to Macao to escape the bubonic plague epidemic that was rampant in Hong Kong from 1894 to 1923.

In this little outpost I was born in the Year of the Tiger, 1914, on the first day of the eighth moon. My mother Chieh, having already produced two sons, heaved a sigh of contentment when the garrulous midwife exclaimed, "Here comes *mui-mui* (little sister)."

The eighth moon in the Chinese calendar was everyone's favorite month. Each night the moon waxed and grew from a sliver to a large yellow globe, and on the fifteenth day (always a full moon in the lunar calendar) there was excitement everywhere.

The Mid-Autumn Festival, or Moon Festival, was our biggest festival after Chinese New Year. We thanked the gods for the year's abundant crops. Tradesmen came to our home to settle all the bills accumulated since the last festival. Beaming children went outdoors in the twilight pulling their paper lanterns on wheels—white paper bunnies, pale green paper carambolas (starfruit), or other tropical fruits—each one aglow with a lit candle inside. Children with their innocent eyes looked up at the moon to see the shadowy rabbit,[4] then joined their little friends to parade along the street. Their sweet voices rang out in the warm summer air, "Moon bright, bright, whole earth alight, new year's eve, betel nut delight." They sang on and on, full of comical allusions, the last word of each line giving them clues to the next.

On the evening of the festival, the two altar tables in our little prayer room were covered with red cloth and food was placed there for the gods and our ancestors. There were many dishes, but always duck with round slices of chewy taro, soaking in an aromatic sauce of anise, fennel, and cinnamon. Lying spread-eagled on a wooden board, its skin bright red and glistening, its tilted snout partly obscured by a pink paper flower stuck in its mouth, was the main offering: a suckling pig only a few weeks old, slowly barbecued over red hot wood chips. This was brought in from outside.

Food for the gods was vegetarian, often with swatches of jet-black seaweed, which we would not eat as it looked like the cook's long pigtail. Slippery, fresh, creamy soybean "skin." Dried

---

[4] The dark areas near the top of the full moon look somewhat like a rabbit. In one legend, three fairy sages transformed themselves into pitiful old men, and begged for food from a fox, a monkey, and a hare. The fox and the monkey both had food to give to the old men, but the hare, empty-handed, jumped into a blazing fire to offer his own flesh instead. The sages were so touched by the hare's sacrifice and act of kindness that they let him live in the Moon Palace, where he became the "Jade Rabbit." Source: "Mid-Autumn Festival," *Wikipedia*. Retrieved 12/1/08.

mushrooms sprinkled with ginger juice and salt, then steamed. Cloud ears—fungus gathered from forest trees—soaked till quadruple their size, then simmered in broth until soft but still crunchy. "Watch out," eldest brother Dick would say, as we chased the pale lemon gingko fruit in the soup. "One in ten thousand is poisonous." We were impressed, but eating the soup did not seem much of a gamble.

Along the edge of the altar table was rice wine in tiny porcelain cups. When it came to my turn to kowtow I would take one of the cups and quickly pour it onto the floor in a sweeping motion. It emitted a sickly sweet smell.

Incense sticks and sandalwood chips smoldering in their own ashes sent spirals of gray smoke to the ceiling. The perfume of white ginger flowers and overripe Manila mangos was so penetrating that the gods and our forebears must have noticed. Surely they were smiling.

Born two weeks before the Moon Festival, I was introduced to our world two weeks after it when I was one month old. Chieh dressed me in pink silk with a simple little cap to match, all lovingly stitched by her. On the cap was sewn a laughing Buddha, made of gold leaf. Friends and relatives gave me *lai see* (little red paper packets) printed with propitious sayings and drawings representing long life and happiness. Inside was tucked a coin or two.

Visitors were served a taste of sweet-tart pigs' trotters with chunks of young ginger, black molasses and vinegar. There was also chicken soup containing wood ear (a fungus similar to cloud ear) and rice wine. Wood ear is wonderfully crunchy and cleans out cholesterol. We all liked this soup, which is especially nourishing for a nursing mother, and served it often throughout our lives.

We lived in Macao for a few years; Father commuted to Hong Kong, and the older brothers went to school there. We lived on the second floor of an apartment house near the remaining facade of St. Paulo Basilica. Chieh said our building was very modern in those days. We paid HK$16 rent per month. There were two sections in the apartment. Ah Ma, the first wife, lived in the other section.

We had two meals a day, but taking care of the children made Chieh hungry most of the time. She would quietly go down to the street to buy a bowl of wonton noodles for three cents. Chieh breast-fed each of her babies for more than two years.

Living in Macao was peaceful, and my earliest memory was a happy one. One hot summer's night with not a whisper of a breeze, Chieh unrolled a straw mat on the veranda floor and said my little sister and I could stay out there for a while. We fanned each other clumsily, producing more beads of sweat on our foreheads. As we paused we heard from the street the sound of wooden sticks clacking together. It was not the street vendor of the sweet red bean soup or the cold tofu "flower", that most tender of sugared fresh bean curd. We called to Chieh, "The wonton seller is here, please, may we have some?" So we went to sleep filled with "swallowed clouds."

Sometimes when I hear the loud roar of an engine, I am back in Macao climbing awkwardly into the sidecar of a motorcycle. The drivers wore uniforms and Ah Ma, with three little ones, had been invited to afternoon tea with His Excellency, the Governor of Macao. Sister and I sat in one vehicle and mother, Father, and fourth brother Wing Sum (J.S.) squeezed into a second one. It must have taken all of ten seconds to roar down our hill to the Praya Grande, then along the water's edge to the Governor's Mansion. It was winter and sunny, and my sister and I wore padded silk clothes that blended well with the pastel colors of the homes of this Portuguese Colony.

Before I could toddle, Chieh took me to our native village Sun Wui in China to see my grandparents. Father had her visit his parents frequently. It was only a few hours north by ferry from Macao to Gong Moon where we disembarked. On the last stretch of the journey, Chieh hired a *sampan*, the size of a long narrow rowboat whose name fittingly meant "three planks." We glided peacefully along one of the waterways that criss-crossed the delta. We had gone hardly an hour when black clouds loomed from the southeast, and winds traveling at high speed bore down on us. The oarsman tried to batten down, hoping to save the flimsy bamboo cover over our heads, but all of it blew away. The wind turned gale force, sometimes pushing from behind and then lashing into our faces. The river looked angry, forcing our sampan to lurch skyward and then crash down. How we ever survived was a miracle! (Chieh would get agitated whenever she relived this episode.) A devout Buddhist, Chieh cried out in supplication to Buddha, "Save life, save life." The oarsman crouched low on the stern hanging on for his life, and with his single oar tied to the stern, tried to keep us from spinning helplessly around. Chieh always finished the telling of our near-tragedy with a giggle.

When we finally reached Sun Wui village, grandfather asked her what I was called. She replied, with my crying still ringing in her ears, "Aaa Nui." Grandfather was profoundly disturbed and asked, "She is mute?" This shows how perplexing our Cantonese dialect can be with its many tones. Chieh meant that I was making the "Aaa-aaa" crying sounds, while Grandfather thought it was the word for mute, which sounds like "Aaa" with a slightly different tone. "Nui" means girl.

Baby boys' names can be really silly, for a reason. They are called "pig," "dog," "cow" and other creatures. The parents are trying to fool the evil one from taking them away. Hair on toddlers would be braided to stick up on top of their heads so that parents could hold on when their little ones were being snatched up to goodness knows where.

Grandfather later named me Sun Ying and elder sister was Sun Wah, because he had attended a Chinese opera starring these two dashing historic heroines. Later all of my six sisters had the prefix of "Sun" added to their names. But my name Sun Ying was rarely used. When I later received my English name, Ansie, my family used that instead. Perhaps they thought using a foreign name launched me into a New World. It's a pity; Sun Ying has such a lilt to it.

The last time my mother, Chieh and I relived this adventure was in 1985 at her apartment in Hong Kong. She lived in one of our family apartment buildings, Caroline Mansions, with an adjoining open verandah in the front leading into my sister Joyce's flat where she and her husband, K.S. Auyang, and their children lived. In the back of Chieh's prayer room was a large garden that was really the top of a lower building next door, also belonging to our family.

She was constantly surrounded by her children and grand-children, dogs (very unusual for a Chinese, but she loved having pets) and cats. Second Brother was the most filial, visiting her daily and fulfilling her slightest wish. She was full of joy when a granddaughter sent her a present from England, and she would savor the thought and love that came with these gifts from so far away. Chieh, being the most unselfish of souls, needed very little to be happy. She told us to be "frugal with oneself but generous with others."

Chieh smoked all her life, tamping tobacco into the spout of her enamel water pipe, then lighting it every time she drew the smoke from the tobacco. Lighting the pipe was a challenge that all of her own children mastered. It was so satisfying to see the red end of the "paper spill"—a rolled paper taper—burst into flames when you blew on it.

Our sweet mother was small and slight, her gray hair combed back in a bob, having a few years earlier decided there was hardly enough hair to make a ladylike bun. It was just before her dinner during my last visit with her when my mother relived her journey to our village. She sat by her mahjong table with a plate of savory snacks and a small drink in her hand.

Chieh, Ansie's mother

I was sad that I lived so far away in California, but many years before, a friend had looked at my palm and said, "You are blessed, Ansie; you will be at your Mother's side when she dies."

Soon after our chat about our long-ago adventure to the village, Chieh was taken to the French Hospital in Hong Kong. On December 14, 1985, when all other family members had gone for lunch, Chieh sat beside her bed and finished her entire meal, even drinking up her bowl of soup. I told her she was a very good girl. Her head dropped and, without another sound, she died peacefully, almost one hundred years old.

CHAPTER 4
OUR HONG KONG HOME

China ceded the island of Hong Kong to Britain in 1842. The land was barren except for a few areas of virgin forest. There was not even any grassland. When Lord Palmerston, the Foreign Minister, reported what the Chinese Emperor had ceded to Great Britain, Queen Victoria was not amused.

This piece of rock broke off from the South China coast aeons past. It had an area of thirty-two square miles, irregular in shape, with the longest part measuring around ten miles. The width varied from two to five miles. On the north shore, facing the mainland, the land rose steeply out of the water to 1,800 feet, which the British named Victoria Peak. In former years Chinese junks sailed to this safe haven to collect water that tumbled down the boulders. They called the area Heung Gong (fragrant harbor). The English adopted it and the name Hong Kong was born.

In 1860, eighteen years later, the Convention of Peking increased the total land by giving the Colony the tip of the Kowloon Peninsula, a mere three and one-quarter square miles.

Thus, Great Britain legally possessed only thirty-five and one-quarter square miles of land.

In 1898, more land was leased, note, *leased*, by the British from China. An official publication stated the area as 270 square miles, plus another seventy-five square miles of the surrounding islands. The total area of the Colony was now almost 391 square miles. The lease was for ninety-nine years. When in 1997 the lease was up, even the lands given to Britain by China were handed back to the Chinese government.

Immediately below the Peak, the British started to build their town, which was named after their Queen Victoria. Old paintings showed the formally dressed English and the Chinese, mostly laborers with their long hair braided, going about their jobs. The water of the harbor lapped nearby as there was little foreshore. To increase the amount of much-needed land facing the harbor, the government poured landfill along its shoreline. One of my early memories was the noise of gongs being beaten loudly and with urgency. Immediately afterward, an explosion shook mounds or hillocks moving the rocks and boulders apart. This occurred at noon and 5 p.m. every day. The British Government was leveling the foothills and blasting rocks to mix with the soil. It was a slow job.

It took twenty years before the Hong Kong government started planting trees, mostly local pines, above the town. Their efforts to beautify Victoria met with unexpected problems. Chinese banyan trees with their widespread canopies were chosen to create relief from the tropical sun. They could endure harsh weather. To produce another tree, one just had to saw off a thick branch and pop it into a hole. Within a few years the lusty roots strangled the town's drainpipes and gave the Sanitary Department headaches. Then candlenut and royal poinciana took the banyan's place.

Today, however, there seems to be no place for shade trees in the town.

During World War I, Father bought land on a hill for our home in Hong Kong. Along the lower end of our property, Palmer & Turner, a British architectural firm, built a very high retaining wall wrapping around a shoulder of the hill. When this was filled, it created a flat area on the top with ample space for a mansion but not much else given the slope of the hill behind it. However, the rest of the property was not left as a hill, but terraced in tiers with concrete walls to brace each flat area. It was not steep, so young and old could manage the many paths and steps. But everyone was young then!

Our house was on the eastern stretch of Kennedy Road. This road started above the edge of the town of Victoria, hugging the hill and passing above the British Army's explosives storage. It continued all the way to the end of an area called Wanchai (Small Bay).

In 1920 we moved from Macao to Dai Uk (Big House), as we called our new home. We had lovely views from all sides. Junks tacked through the narrow Laimun Channel (*laimun* means fish gate), into the spacious "Fragrant Harbor." Steamers from all over the world dropped anchor, hoisting the British flag to fly alongside their own countries' colors. And, of course, plenty of sampans scurried by to service the steamers anchored in midstream.

Below us on the east side of the house was a Chinese temple. We never went near the temple, as the Buddhist nuns called up ghosts in anguished voices while whacking the ground with matting. Their shrill wailing filled our small valley. This was infrequent, but too scary to forget.

Distant View of Mr. Lee Hy-san's residence.

Our house, "Dai Uk" on Kennedy Road, Hong Kong

We did not mind the daily early morning greeting of Uncle Luk, whose resounding "Jo-Sun" (good morning) woke us up. He was doing his morning walk on Bowen Path, half way up the hill. Uncle Luk, who had worked in California, owned the laundry at the nearby curve of Kennedy Road where rainwater tumbled down from the crease in the hill into a *nullah* (water drain). On sunny days his workers spread bed sheets from the British military barracks onto the rocks to bleach and dry. I wonder if some young British soldier, so far from home, ever delighted in the fresh scent of the strong sun on his cotton sheets.

Sixth sister Amy and Ansie
in garden of Dai Uk c. 1923

The roosters from a neighboring house joined in the morning chorus. Fortunately, there was never more than one or two. Whenever I hear one, my thoughts immediately fly back to those years.

A few large homes hugged the opposite side of our valley. Close to them, a rock wall rose straight up to Bowen Road. During heavy rains, a wide waterfall came tumbling down. Light showers produced billowing sprays.

Behind Dai Uk was a garden that father had created. There was a Peking pavilion with every detail correct. The red pillars stayed bright for many years. A short path led to a fountain against a painted wall scene. On the other side of the house, looking towards town, was an intriguing miniature mountain with dwellings and people. At the base was a "lake" with real goldfish. Further on was a large bamboo bower covered with creepers. There were porcelain barrel stools where one could sit and chat, read a book, or bite into a fragrant guava from a nearby tree.

The Peking pavilion in the Dai Uk garden

Dai Uk was designed with the ground floor devoted to entertaining, with a music room and a large library of Chinese books and a comfortable sofa. We had a baby grand piano and later a pianola, a new invention that played music by itself using punched paper rolls. The main living room contained only blackwood furniture, which is fine if you are used to such austere supports for your body. There were no cushions.

Sometimes Father would allow the children to attend his parties for his English friends at Dai Uk. I remember how much I enjoyed them even though I did not understand a word anyone said. I loved the way the pink Venetian glass lights in the ceiling made our faces rosy. There were two Italian marble figures on stands. Rounded porcelain flower pots with palms and flowering shrubs helped to make the hot summer nights cooler for the guests. Electric fans also helped. Ah Ma had an English teacher who taught her to say, "Don't mention it" after a "Thank you." Quite a tongue-twister for her. In those days the English never used "You're welcome," which would have been easier to pronounce.

From the ground floor, a large center staircase took us to the next floor. Here Father and Ah Ma lived with their children, second sister Doris, fourth brother Wing Sum (J.S.), and fifth sister Dione. Harold, third brother, was in England at school.

I lived with my own mother Chieh, with second brother Ming Hop, and two younger sisters, Joyce and Amy. We were on the top floor. My brother Dick, the eldest, was in England at school.

The main kitchen at the back of the ground floor was large, with a male cook and helpers. They produced the rice, soup, vegetable and other dishes. Ah Ma did not like the rice flour bought at the shop. She thought it was not good enough, so she installed a long wood treadle in a retaining wall in the garden for pounding rice to make super fine flour. The mortar and pestle were made of solid stone.

The cooks provided meals for the family and staff, which included the five gardeners. However, the Sikh guards provided their own meals, and had living quarters in the garden. The guards, brothers Kata Singh and Nam Singh, were so faithful, they seemed like part of the family. Indeed, when their sons grew up they also became guards for the family.

On the first floor was another kitchen for all the extra foods we enjoyed. At 10 a.m. and 5 p.m. the family gathered in a small dining room. There were always one or more cousins there. If there was a crowd, the male cousins would gather at another table in some other part of the house. One cousin was great at math and helped me with my homework.

We had an outstanding cook, who was, of all things, a vegetarian! One of my beloved sisters, fifth sister Dione, later became a superb cook and was very generous. She loved Henry, my husband, and always had him sit next to her so that she could ply him with plenty of everything.

Even in our growing up days, until I left home to work in China in 1939, there was no electricity or running water. Everyday down in Wanchai there would be lines of people with 5-gallon tins, waiting their turn for water at the street pumps.

When third brother Harold came back from Oxford University, he used one level of the garden at Dai Uk as a tennis court. Weekend tennis with friends was always wonderful, even if one did not always play. Sister Doris or cousin Ping made tea. This always meant sandwiches and cakes, fresh fruit and sweets and strong English tea with milk and sugar. We sat on the flat roof of a small storeroom to watch some of the Colony's best players. I might mention a B team, which was kid brother J.S. who had tennis friends, and me, usually the only girl player (they graciously accepted me as one of the boys). I learned if I stood way behind the line, I could usually return their killing serves.

Higher up the hill was the largest flat area. Here were some playthings for children, but mostly it was for the gardeners as a staging ground for the myriad potted plants that adorned not only the grounds, but the verandas of the house too. Here Ah Ma would plant some favorite vegetables. We had no trees except for one or two papaya trees which my mother Chieh planted. They were miniature but bore sweet fruit. Looking at them, they were hardly large enough to be called trees. Ah Ma did not relish the spirits that live in trees.

At the very top of the property, Father very wisely built another building with six spacious apartments and called it the Lee Building. It had enormous rooms and very high ceilings. It was cool throughout the hot summers. A few apartments were at first rented or used as homes by friends of the family. Then when Father took on more concubines (three in all), each concubine had a floor in Lee Building where she lived with her children. Later when we were grown we used it for ourselves. Henry, my husband, and I made it our home after he retired from Citibank and had other work in Hong Kong. It was a wonderful place to live. Thank you, Father.

The new "Lee Building" near to the main residence.

Lee Building at the top of the property

The Lee Hysan Family household c. 1923
Ansie is in the front row, center

Sister Doris on left with Ansie
Dai Uk garden, Hong Kong c. 1923

CHAPTER 5
CHILDHOOD IN HONG KONG

When I was about eight or nine years old, Sister Doris and I entered the Diocesan Girls' School (DGS) in Kowloon, a Star Ferry ride across the lovely Hong Kong harbor to the mainland where a rounded piece of land met the water—the "Peninsula." The school was started by the Church of England for Eurasian and Chinese children who wanted to study English. There was one for boys, too, the DBS.

When the English headmistress interviewed us, she told Father that we needed English names at school, and she gave him two. When we returned home he put the names in a hat. Elder sister pulled out "Doris," and I, "Ansie." Father had a present for each name; mine was a pendant from Europe made with tiny diamonds on a platinum chain. I still have it.

Diamond pendant from Father

Most of us had a hard time making an "R" sound, so "Doris" was not used at home. "Ansie" was easy to say, and since no one ever used "Sun Ying'" anyway, I became Ansie to them, and my baby name was not used. It was forbidden to call anyone by their name if they were older, even by a few months, so "Third Sister" I remained to my younger siblings.

I can remember many little details of that day. We were in Father's bedroom with his enormous four-poster bed. It was draped all around with white gauze, so flimsy that the air from the electric fan would flow through, yet no eyes could pry inside. During the day the front of these drapes were parted and secured by large decorative clasps.

There was a quaint carved chair, in blackwood, shaped like the letter S, for a couple to sit on opposite sides. I think it was copied from the French love seat, where one could execute a warm embrace, and that was as far as one could go. The carvings were typically Cantonese; ornate.

Father's bedroom with four-poster bed
and S-shaped love seat on left

We were boarders at the DGS in Kowloon, a short bus ride from the Star Ferry on the mainland. Every weekend Ah Ma would visit us, bringing chicken soup in a thermos bottle. We would go to a corner of the limited school grounds and drink the soup, scorching hot from the thermos flask. (To this day, I believe the Chinese thermos keeps liquids hotter than any other kind of container.) We stayed two terms at DGS, and were still much too shy to speak any English.

The Misses Doris and Ansie Loos starting for the Diocesan girl School from home.

Ansie, Doris and Fourth Brother J.S. with Father
on front steps of Dai Uk c.1923

Then in 1924, when I was only nine years old, Father decided to send Doris and me to school in England. It really was unheard of to be sending such young Chinese girls for schooling so far away. Ready or not, we were going to be shipped off halfway around the world to a country of which we had never heard, and with a chaperone, a Miss Turner, whom Father had just met.

Father had instructed us not to tell anyone about our separate mothers. In Hong Kong, as in China, it was then legal to have concubines. Since only the wealthy could afford such a household, it meant that vast numbers of offspring had good nutrition and a better education. All the children in a family called the wife Mother, and no Chinese would ever be insensitive enough to ask which of the household's women was her (or his) biological mother. Father, ever thoughtful, had a solution for inquisitive people abroad. Passports were needed. He went to register our births. Since Doris and I were born the same year and only eight months apart, he recorded my birthday as two years later.

My birth certificate states that I was born on August 29, 1916. Not true. My birthday was the first day of the eighth moon in 1914, or September 20, 1914 in the Western calendar. But I was stuck with the 1916 date all my life. From then on I had to be two years younger. The birth certificate also states that my mother is Wong Lan Fong, or Ah Ma, the first mother. Again, not true, as my real mother was Chieh, the first concubine.[5]

There was only one instance when Doris and I were asked directly if we had different mothers. This was by our guardian in England. Both of us stood dumbfounded and, not meaning to be rude, grew red in the face and remained tongue-tied, remembering what Father had told us.

The spring of 1924 was a sad one for Ah Ma. She wept bitterly as she did not want us to leave home, but Father would not be swayed. Secretly, my own mother Chieh told me later that she was truly happy for me. Auntie Zimmern, a Eurasian friend, guided Ah Ma to Whiteaway Laidlaw department store to buy wool undies, saying to be sure to get large sizes. They shrank alarmingly at the very first wash. Our sewing amah (servant) made padded clothes for us using thin layers of raw silk that we produced at home.

---

[5] The birth certificate also states that I was born in Hong Kong, when in fact I was born in Macao.

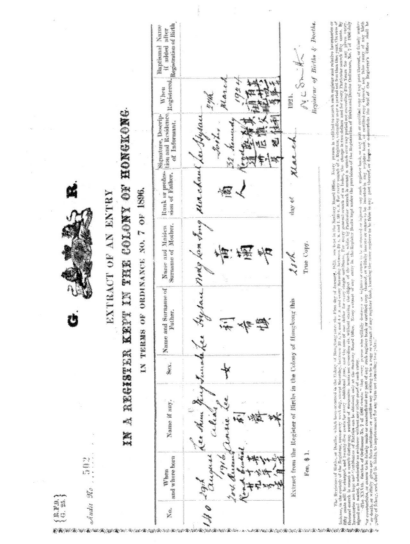

My birth certificate, issued in 1924, states that I was born on
August 29, 1916, when the actual date was September 30, 1914.
Wong Lan Fong, (Ah Ma, the first mother), is listed as my mother
and not Chieh, my real mother, who was the first concubine.

Doris, Father and Ansie
Hong Kong c. 1923

At that time we had a hobby of raising silkworms in flat round rattan baskets. It was fun listening to them munching day and night on mulberry leaves. After a month of eating, the worms emitted strands of silk (to the remarkable length of half a mile), winding the thread around themselves to form a cocoon. We collected the cocoons and took them to a shop straight down a steep hill (*so many steps*) to Wanchai. The silk carding shop was wide open to the street during most of the year. Inside was a large wooden frame gleaming with bent wire teeth set in rows. A man stripped to the waist used his bare feet to pump on the treadle. Eventually, after steaming and other processes, the contents of the cocoons were teased into puffs of the lightest silk, like white spun sugar. We used to pad our winter silk clothes with the thinnest layer of this spun silk.

Inside the steamer trunks Ah Ma tucked in boxes of salted calamansi (Philippine lime) for sore throats, chewy ginger for seasickness, stinging Tiger Balm ointment for forehead or tummy to ease aches and pains. There were pretty tin caddies of dried petals of chrysanthemum, egg yellow frangipani and jasmine, to be brewed as teas. These infusions cooled off the heat created by eating fried or spicy foods.

The memory of the spring day we left home stands out clearly in my mind. Our ship was anchored midstream in the Hong Kong harbor and I followed Elder Sister (it took me a while to be bold enough to call Doris by her name) up the steep ladder, my hands barely able to grasp the thick rope strung along the sides. I kept my eyes up, avoiding any downward glances at the sea below. With a sigh of relief I reached the deck only to be assailed by a smell of cooked cabbage coming out of a vent. The color of the superstructure added to my sick feeling. It was a horrid yellow. Our ship, the SS *City of York*, belonged to the Peninsula & Orient line (P&O), which was referred to by the British themselves as the "Putrid and Orful."

Father, Ah Ma, younger brother J.S. and a camera crew came to bid us farewell. As the family left, we took out our large white handkerchiefs (supplied by Father for this purpose) and waved for the movie camera as the family sped away in a motor launch. Doris had already used hers for wiping her tears, but I was far too excited to be sad. How could I know that this would be the last time I would see Father?

Miss Turner, the woman who took care of us on the steamer, was English, a visiting journalist. We met her the night before we boarded the ship. Little did she realize we were obedient children so her job was easy. The only time she lost her temper was at the beginning of the voyage while the ship was headed for Singapore.

After the children's supper of starchy foods and overcooked vegetables (sometimes there was rice but it was sweet and called rice pudding), Miss Turner told us to go to our cabin. We had a tiny inside room with blowers for ventilation and when there was a following wind, the air would be smoky. "POSH" did not apply to our cabin, "Port Out, Starboard Home." The cooler, more desirable, side of the ship was on the port side when coming out to the Far East and on the starboard side when going home.

It was stifling and we were sweating and thirsty. So we rang the bell. We did this several times at polite intervals. Miss Turner came charging in and asked us not to play with the bell. It could be plainly heard in the dining room, she said. She was obviously ashamed of our behavior. By this time our throats were parched and the thought of not being able to leave the cabin to get a drink was unbearable, so we explained our plight in broken English. Mercifully, the steward was instructed to have a carafe of water in the cabin at all times.

The SS *City of York* crossed the Bay of Bengal and we were glad to get off in Colombo, Ceylon, to run around on the long wide sandy beach called Mount Lavinia next to the famous hotel by that name. Any handbag left opened on the beach would be plundered by large black birds that would pick up anything shiny and take it to their keepers in the nearby jungle.

It remained hot as the ship stopped at Aden and then steamed into the still air of the Red Sea, through the Suez Canal to Port Said. Doris and I were thrilled with the gully-gully [6]man who came on board. He did wonderful sleight of hand tricks and never

---

[6] A gully-gully man was a once popular Egyptian magician/conjuror who commonly boarded ships passing through the Suez Canal. His name was derived from the "gulla-gulla-gulla" incantation he chanted as he performed his tricks.

stopped talking with his singsong voice, beguiling young and old alike.

We slipped into the Mediterranean and felt cool at last. That was short-lived. No sooner had we rounded the Straits of Gibraltar into the Bay of Biscay than we ran into biting winds. Our boat pitched and rolled and I was seasick again. At long last we arrived at Southampton, England.

CHAPTER 6
SCHOOL IN ENGLAND:
1924-1928

It had been more than a month since we had left home. How strange to walk on land with the pavements feeling like they were heaving! We took a train with Miss Turner to Victoria Station in London, and then changed to Paddington Station. We hugged Miss Turner good-bye and hopped onto another train for Oxford. On board was a fatherly conductor keeping an eye on us. "Ere's where you gets off young ladies," he said with his strange English as the train came to a stop.

It was about nine in the evening, but since it was early summer the sun seemed unwilling to sink below the horizon and instead cast a golden glow over beautiful Oxford. On the platform stood a tall, handsome man, and with him a beautiful boy of about twelve years old, with curly blond hair. "Here they are, Dad," the boy said. Then, taking our small pieces of luggage (our steamer trunks were forwarded from Southampton), the lad introduced himself. "I'm Buster and this is my Dad, Mr. Churchill."

After shaking hands we had the choice of taking a taxi or a horse-drawn carriage. We chose the latter and with a crack of the whip, the coachman urged his nag into a slow trot. We clip-clopped over the cobblestones and saw the spires and turrets of the colleges of Oxford. Their outlines stood out sharply in the twilight. "Oh, what's that?" I asked Mr. Churchill, pointing at a dark figure with a long pole. Buster replied, "He's the lamplighter doing his rounds. When dusk comes he lights all the street lamps." Then he turned to us and said quite simply, "Dad's blind. Didn't you know?" We were astonished, as Mr. Churchill had looked so normal and walked with such sure steps. We did not notice that he had Buster's arm at the station. Before Mr. Churchill lost his sight, he had worked for the Hong Kong government as a civil engineer surveying land. Our lawyer, Mr. Beavis of Wilkinson and Grist, recommended him and Mrs. Churchill to be our guardians.

Mr. and Mrs. Churchill
Our guardians at Oxford, England.

Soon we reached 4 Crick Road, Oxford, which was to be our home during school holidays for four years. On the front steps of the three-story house, Mrs. Churchill was waiting to welcome us. She stood tall and slim with an aquiline nose and pointed chin. She wore her hair up, teased at the sides. She gave us each a warm hug and I felt comfortable with her right away.

How can we forget the Churchill household? We were introduced to the cook, Mrs. Lee, and a housemaid. The next morning we met the gardener, Mr. Lee, no relation to the cook. So what with the two little Miss Lees, and our two brothers, Dick and Harold Lee, I doubt in all of England were there so many Lees from different families in one household. It was puzzling, as I did not then know that Lee is a common English surname.

Doris, Harold and Ansie
Oxford c. 1924

Dick, our eldest brother, was then at Pembroke College at Oxford and not living at 4 Crick Road. Harold, not old enough for college, was at Magdalen College School. "Magdalen" was my introduction to the peculiar way the English have with words. In this case it is pronounced "Môd'lin." Harold was moved to a small room in the attic at 4 Crick Road when we came back for the holidays. Here he would amuse himself playing all kinds of jazz on the gramophone or whatever there was for teenagers in those days, surrounding himself with a tangle of wires and percussion instruments. During the holidays, the brothers went to the Continent, although probably not together, as they were so different in taste and temperament.

I often brushed Mrs. Churchill's long fine brown hair, and we quickly developed a bond. I was let off folding the clean laundry as she said I was too young. Apparently Doris was not and I wondered about that until I remembered that officially she was two years older.

Mrs. Churchill was unsure how to dress little girls, so she solved the problem by taking us down to London to a large store and letting a supervisor advise her. We loved those outings. The only dress I remember was a purple frock, quite shapeless, with a long ribbon that hung from each shoulder and that seemed pointless. It was my best and I wore it for many holiday parties. Each time we went to London we saw a play, one being *Charley's Aunt* and another *The Ghost Train*. And of course we dined in fine restaurants.

The Churchills had two other sons, Jack and Tom, both of whom were already in the army. Later, during World War II, "Mad Jack", a decorated Lieutenant-Colonel in the commandos, acquired fame and this affectionate nickname for his heroic

From left: Dick, Ansie, Doris and Harold
Ansie and Doris wearing the dresses with ribbons
Oxford c. 1926

escapades. He would lead his troops wearing kilts and playing the bagpipes. He used his bow and arrow as a deadly weapon.

Jack broke out of two prison camps in Germany by digging tunnels. At one of the camps the Germans nailed him to the floor because they thought he was a relative of Winston Churchill. Later posted in the Adriatic, Jack was again captured. After only forty-eight hours he wrote the German Commander, "You have treated us well. If after the war you are ever in England come and have dinner with me and my wife." [7]

Tom became a Major General and served as a staff officer. We met again after the war when he was posted in Singapore.

Buster joined the Fleet Air Arm, the elite group of the armed forces. Tragically, he was listed as missing in the Mediterranean early in the war in 1940.

Buster went to the Dragon School, which was fairly near our house. During the holidays he and his friends would play card games with us in the basement. Years later a naval officer stationed in Hong Kong said, "You and Doris always won at cards. How did you two do it?" I assured him it was pure luck.

The family must have had fun papering the walls of this room with cartoons and drawings from newspapers and magazines. One of the cartoons had a haughty Englishman saying, "Chop chop" (pidgin English for "hurry up") to a bent rickshaw-puller as he strained like a beast of burden. The Cantonese used to call all whites *gweilo* ("foreign devils"). Some still do, but only because of common usage and not maliciously.

Miss Turner had invited us to go to Yorkshire that first summer and she rented a large farmhouse. Doris and I took a train. Looking back I am quite astonished by the way we two young Chinese girls could travel without any thought of danger. How the world has changed.

The vastness of the moors in Yorkshire was exciting. Though Hong Kong had plenty of open space, it was up steep hills or straight down to the sea. In the English countryside we could look to the horizon, covered with yellow gorse and purple heather. We went for walks and picnics and I had my first pony ride.

---

[7] This quote comes from Mad Jack's obituary, of which I have a photocopy. It is missing source information.

The farmer's wife cooked for us, and she would dig potatoes. We Cantonese called these tubers Holland potatoes and we sautéed them thinly sliced with pork, and never used them as a staple. Frequent trips to the beach enriched our suppers with the fishermen's catch: mussels, cockles, crabs and different bright-eyed fish. We thought all beaches had fine golden sand like Repulse Bay and Shek-O in Hong Kong, but it was not so. Here the sea lapped or crashed onto pebbles and rocks that took on glistening dark hues. On calm sunny days we stepped gingerly along the shore, picking up shells and hoping the crabs would not nip our toes. We did not swim there.

Twice a week during summer holidays with the Churchills, Doris and I dutifully selected two biscuits, ginger snaps being my favorite, and walked to the bathing place on the River Char to take swimming lessons in the freezing water. I think in those days the breaststroke and backstroke were the only ways to swim. The crawl was for Australians. We learned to dive, nothing fancy, but to enter the water without doing belly flops. This sounds simple but the water was always pitch black and cold. I could never see the bottom. The whole exercise was, to put it mildly, unpleasant.

On sunny afternoons we had tea at home under the pear trees in the back garden. We buttered small scones and the bees would buzz around the homemade jam. Sandwiches made of thin white bread with "mustard and cress" tucked between the slices were entirely new to our taste buds. There was always simple sponge cake or a dark fruitcake. We drank tea, very strong, with milk and sugar. We would admire the rock garden, which we helped build, and how little plants peeped out of the crevices. Squirrels romped about and robins teased our cat. Those lazy warm afternoons remain a pleasant memory.

Once Jack Churchill came home and we went punting on the river, packing a picnic lunch to enjoy on the banks under a shady tree. I tried to propel this flat-bottomed boat with the long wooden pole, but it was too heavy for me. The river was shallow so that you moved the boat by standing up on the front end and pushing the pole down onto the river bed and walking to the other end, or was it vice-versa?

Summer holidays over, Mrs. Churchill enrolled us in the Headington Hill School, a bus ride from home. But that did not even last one term. In Hong Kong Mrs. Beavis, the wife of our family lawyer, had arranged for us to attend Moira House at Eastbourne in Sussex. There had been a misunderstanding.

At Moira House, Miss Ingham, the daughter of the school founder, was the headmistress and Miss Swann and Miss Tizzard (E.T.) were senior staff. Miss Swann always taught us in the assembly hall, training our voices (for speaking, not singing), and Miss Tizzard was in charge of most of the other classes for the juniors. We were taught French by Madame Posniakoff, and art in a spacious studio by an American artist. There were several piano teachers and in every bedroom stood a piano as we all practiced every day. We said grace before meals, then were served plates of food with comical nicknames. There were about ninety boarders and a few day scholars and no other Chinese in the school at that time. The one Indian girl, Raji, later became the Maharani of Indore.

No child could have had more fun at school than I did. We had no exams, not even the seniors, and no uniforms. Piano lessons were part of the school curriculum and most of the girls played a second instrument. I would listen with longing to the evening concerts once a week, my ears on the floor as the school orchestra played below my room after my bedtime. Classical music was magical and it was completely new to us. Doris had chosen the violin and was soon playing in the orchestra, but I was too young to join them. Later, I took up the cello and played at the school concert. The piece was completely tuneless and I was embarrassed, but I was given loud applause. Every Wednesday evening we had ballet classes finishing off with ballroom dancing, at which time the older girls entered the dance class. I was doing the Charleston and the tango and everything else in between.

Another class was called Dalcroze, where we exercised to music. Monsieur Dalcroze came over from the Continent to see how our school was faring with his new idea. This was in 1924 and sixty years later, in 1984, I came across a Dalcroze class in Palo Alto, California, near where I now live. The lady I talked to was amazed to meet someone who had actually met Monsieur Dalcroze.

When Doris and I arrived at Moira House, the theme for the whole school was the "Middle Ages." At the school play of *Aucassin and Nicolette*, I was the black sheep among the flock, which made me very proud!

There were so many things to look forward to at school, such as outings to a big hotel by the sea in Eastbourne to listen to Fritz Kreisler play the violin. Every Sunday after supper, we younger ones gathered in the living room to spend an hour with Mr. Ingham, the founder of the school. We wore our best dresses and chatted quietly with each other, awed by the formal sitting room. Mr. Ingham was musical and we always gathered around the piano to sing songs. He was full of praise when we answered his musical quizzes correctly. Settling down in a big armchair with us surrounding him, he read enthralling passages from the classics. It was hard to wait for the next week's installment. Sweets from home were pooled at the beginning of term and every weekday after lunch we could select two pieces to take to our room for a quiet time with a book from the library.

Doris, a classmate and Ansie
Moira House School
c. 1925

We had great athletics at Moira House, plenty of tennis, hockey and rounders (like softball) for the young ones. Our school was the first one to try playing cricket, but it did not catch on.

The Sussex Downs were right behind our school and perfect for walks with Miss Cummings, our gym teacher, and for horseback riding. Mrs. Churchill had taken us to London to have our riding habits made complete. With hard velvet caps, we looked as if we were competing in the Olympics! The other girls wore soft caps and comfortable breeches. Oh, how I envied them. At Beachy Head we could see the English Channel. (Memory chooses to forget blasting cold winds and drifting fog.) We brought apples and carrots for our mounts and it was a surprise to me to have them interact with us, nuzzling at jackets to see what treats we had brought for them and eating from our outstretched hands. One day we joined a group of hunters. As the riders gathered, my horse decided she would play a trick on me and bent down on her forelegs. Before I could collect my wits, she had me over her head (thank goodness for my hard riding cap). The term "I wish the earth would open up and swallow me" was the way I felt.

There was a class called "language." I asked Miss Mona Swann, "Which language?" "The English language," she said. Under her, the school excelled in elocution and year after year the seniors won competitions with other schools. I remember arithmetic was patiently taught, not as a class, but at whatever pace you could manage. I was allowed to join the singing group two years my senior (in fact, my true age) and found the harmonizing sounds of the alto very beautiful.

During school holidays, we were invited by school friends to stay with them. This gave us glimpses of the various ways families lived. At one household we could get up at any time for breakfast and on the buffet table of the dining room there was a spread of silver chafing dishes for ham, bacon, grilled kidneys, sausages, tomatoes. Cut glass jars contained marmalade, lemon curd and jams. The cook would pop in to see if we wanted toast and eggs. One schoolmate was American and her father had crates of oranges shipped from California. Every night, a tall glass of orange juice was placed by our bedside table and we were politely told to drink it in the morning, please. At another home we changed for dinner and played mahjong with the grown-ups after the meal.

In 1923, Rumer Godden,[8] who later became a famous author, entered Moira House. It wasn't long before Miss Swann recognized in Rumer a budding writer and asked her if she would like to omit most of the school curriculum, taking only a few subjects—literature, history, French, and music—and concentrate on her writing skills. Rumer wrote about how hard she worked with Miss Swann guiding her every step. A friend who lives here at The Sequoias, my retirement home in California, told me she had seen my name in Rumer Godden's autobiography published in 1987, *A Time To Dance, No Time To Weep*. When I read the book, I saw the mention of a Chinese girl named "Ansie." But the setting was a school Rumer just hated, not my beloved Moira House. I was really curious and wrote to Rumer through her publisher. She promptly replied:

> Indeed I remember you and Doris at Moira House. Once, when Sister [the matron] was ill I had the pleasure of bathing you! And I often wonder what happened to you. So much is being written about China now. It was good news that you and your husband are so contented in your retirement home and that you have a good library, which makes such a difference. Here, at Ardnacloich we are truly remote so that I can seldom get to one.

---

[8] Margaret Rumer Godden, OBE (1907–1998), was an English author of over 60 works of fiction, poetry, biography and autobiography under the pen name of Rumer Godden. Several of her books have been made into classic films, including *Black Narcissus* (1947) based on the novel published in 1938, and *The River* (1951) directed by Jean Renoir and based on the novel published in 1946. One of her children's books, *The Diddakoi*, won the Whitbread award. Source: "Rumer Godden," *Wikipedia*. Retrieved 1/27/09.

I never went back to Moira House except once to open the new library wing there, which was named after me; a great honor. Mona [Swann] though was a continuing part of my life until the end, and her work seems to go on and on in me. I am most glad you went to see her. She must have loved that. Thank you indeed for writing.

Best wishes,
Rumer

I realize now that Rumer had mistakenly placed me at another school, one she attended just before coming to Moira House. She was seven years my senior, and I too remember her giving me a bath. She was called Peggie then.

Rumer wrote this article for Moira House's publication, *The Shuttle, Centenary Number 1875-1975* (Eastbourne, Moira House, Spring 1975). She had been to four different schools before she arrived at Moira House in 1923:

I hated school—until that morning. Even the prayers were different, not the usual absent-minded muttering and dragging hymns, but something to listen to, think of, and there was a feeling of looking forward, not only in the prayer of St. Paul: 'I count not myself to have apprehended, but this one thing I do: forgetting those things that are behind and reaching forth....' And Miss Ingham was so beautiful, so much at ease, as were the girls. In those days the teaching at Moira House was, for an imaginative girl, inspired; the brain child of Miss Ingham and E.T., [the headmistress and Miss

Tizzard, a teacher], it turned on a three year cycle based on history—not just the history of England as taught in most schools, but world history stretching from the earliest civilization to the present day; as the cycle turned, for instance to the age of Egypt, we were steeped in Egyptian art, poetry, drama, architecture and geography—even the pictures in the school were changed; the same with the Grecian age, the Roman and, as we progressed, we wrote and illustrated our own textbooks which proved, at any rate to me, of infinite value in later years. This system was killed by the examination syllabuses, now compulsory for all schools; and to my infinite regret my daughters never had it, because it was a revelation and there sprang in me a hunger, a famished hunger, for learning; to study, concentrate, work, which, for me, meant write.

My husband Henry and I took our daughter, Vicky, and her husband, Jim Merchant, to Moira House to celebrate its centenary on June 28, 1975. Miss Swann arranged for our hotel and left a card with a picture of a swan to welcome us on our arrival at Eastbourne. We drove up Carlisle Road and, with much anticipation, entered the school I had not seen for fifty years. We signed the Centenary Book, toured the school, and at the hockey field met some of the juniors of those long ago years. There were two faces I could recognize, but not the one who said, "I was your best friend, remember?" They told me that I was the fastest runner up and down the playing field.

Moira House July 1925

I am in the front row, sixth from left.   Sister Doris is in the front row, second from right.
Rumer Godden is middle row, middle right with braids.

Mona Swann became Headmistress after Doris and I left England, and we visited her several times at Eastbourne with Didie Irwin (née Downer). Mona died on August 29, 1991, at the age of 97. At All Saints' Church, Eastbourne, a Service of Thanksgiving for the Life and Work of Mona Swann was attended by many of the Old Girls. The first Reader was Barbara Palmer (whom we juniors admired) with her husband, Bishop Simon Phipps, leading the service. When I read the name of the second Reader, it brought a grin to my face. It was Prunella Scales, the TV wife of John Cleese in *Fawlty Towers*. Her mother was my schoolmate, Catherine Scales, known as Bimbo during our school years.

Doris and Ansie at Oxford

Was I ever blessed to have Doris as my sister. She was so good to me that I never once resented her looking so beautiful. She had fair skin and roses in her cheeks, an unusual complexion for a

Cantonese. Straight white teeth behind dainty red lips. She must have been a throwback to a Northern princess. Not only in looks but also in our demeanor we were worlds apart. She was secretive, reserved and suffered (in later years) in silence. I poured my heart out to anyone who would listen, and I was a tomboy. The first term at Moira House one of the girls said to me in disbelief, "You are her sister?" To top it all she was intelligent. Later, when we were back in Hong Kong at DGS, she graduated first in her class, was Head girl of the school and also captain of our netball (basketball) team. But I was never jealous of her because of her sweet nature. Whenever anyone gave us presents, she would let me choose first.

On April 30, 1928, during Easter holidays at Oxford in our fourth year in England, my sister woke me up and spoke. "Ansie, I have had a strange dream, but I was really awake," she said. "Father came to me and said, 'Don't be frightened, everything will be all right.' He was so real that I reached out to touch him, but he disappeared. Whatever does he mean?"

"What did he look like?" I asked, my head half covered by the eiderdown, as the house was chilly. She did not answer.

After we dressed, I hurried downstairs to watch Mr. Churchill light the fire in the dining room. As he was totally blind, I was fascinated to see him do this job with such self-confidence. He set a match to the paper in the grate, and when he heard the kindling flare up, he placed a large rectangular piece of metal over the whole fireplace. Slowly the draft made a roaring sound and the wood chips caught fire, at which point he removed the metal piece and the rush of air subsided, leaving little tongues of flame licking at the coals.

After breakfast, Mrs. Churchill said to Doris, who was still disturbed by seeing Father, "Whatever is the matter with you this morning?" To cheer Doris up, she said, "After we sort out the laundry, you and Ansie can walk to the tuck shop." It was always such a treat to go there to choose some sweets. After the meal I offered to read the newspaper to Mr. Churchill in his smoking room while Doris put away the clean laundry.

That day was sunny but cold, so we tucked a wooly scarf under our coats and walked to the shop. Our weekly pocket money was not always on sweets, but sometimes on children's magazines that had exciting stories and hilarious comics. We stayed as long as we dared at the shop (reading as fast as we could) and finally bought a thin paperback that had puzzles and games. Returning home, we peered over fences to see the early spring blooms along the way. Before we could ring the doorbell Mrs. Churchill was there.

"Come in children and go to the drawing room." We took off our coats and thought someone was visiting us. In the drawing room was Mr. Churchill who handed his wife a sheet of paper. His face was grave. "Sit down dears, I'm afraid it is bad news." Gracious, what could it be? Perhaps Mother had decided to veto any more riding lessons. With trembling voice Mrs. Churchill read the telegram, "Please inform Dick, Harold, Doris and Ansie that their father died today. It was an accident. Return home immediately." Doris started to sob right away. From the moment father was killed, she already knew, for his spirit came to comfort her. I could not comprehend anything at all and was dry-eyed.

It was a horrible shock for everyone. The school had to be informed. Then Dick and Harold had a busy time going to steamship companies. The first available ship sailed from Marseilles, an NYK ship (Nippon Yusan Kaisha), the SS *Katori Maru*. All kinds of vaccinations against all sorts of tropical illnesses had to be arranged. Also, my dentist adjusted those torturing wooden pegs to push my teeth straight.

We stayed a few days in Paris where I bought my first handbag. I was so train sick going to Marseilles that my torturing braces went down the toilet and I was so relieved that Doris and I had fits of laughter. Good riddance!

There was a delay of several days in Marseilles so we sampled delicious bouillabaisse and went often to the movies. French films were rather different from "Peter Pan," and our gentle guardians in England would have raised their eyebrows. But we did see some American films. I fell in love with Gary Cooper in his first film, "The Winning of Barbara Worth." I was quite struck by the lanky young lad who adored the heroine from afar. He made a great sacrifice for her but did not get his gal.

Finally, we boarded the ship and slowly steamed through the Mediterranean. We saw a different gully-gully man in Port Said, and continued on through the narrow passage of the Suez Canal to Ceylon and Singapore.

At Singapore we were guests of a Chinese family whose daughter studied law in England and had a crush on Brother Dick. Their garden stood on the edge of the sea, and I was so thrilled to see what I thought was the most perfect pale yellow moon hanging over the horizon. Then I realized there were other "moons" all around. Even now my thoughts fly back to that Singapore garden when I see a similar outdoor light.

My mind is a blank as to our arrival at Hong Kong harbor, but I remember the moment we climbed up the steps to the side gate of the grounds to 32 Kennedy Road. I was thirteen years old and had been away from home for four years.

CHAPTER 7
HONG KONG AND PEKING:
1928-1939

Home at last, Dick, Harold, Doris and I walked up a flight of stone steps and entered the side gate of the grounds. It was a scorching afternoon. Our Sikh guard, Kata Singh, looking smart and erect in his uniform topped by a white turban, greeted us with obvious pleasure. His young son and nephew, with big grins on their handsome faces, stood behind him. However, our warm welcome was cut short when a tall lean stranger barred our way and handed us unbleached calico robes with pointed hoods and told us to put them on top of our clothes.

I could hear a hum of voices from the house but could not imagine what was happening. Father had been dead for almost two months. This man, master of ceremonies I supposed, told us to proceed to the house on our knees. *On our knees?* The gowns were floor-length and impeded our forward movement, though they did protect us from the hot ground. We managed to get up the wide front steps, our faces bathed in beads of sweat mingled with our tears. Trembling with apprehension, we entered the large reception room of our home.

The big reception hall was packed with people. Incense smoke stung my eyes. Where were Chieh, my own mum, Ah Ma, my official mother, the third and fourth mothers, and all my younger siblings? On the left were two rows of women on their knees, wailing. A few looked up but I could not see any family faces. I learned later the women were paid mourners. Yellow-robed priests chanted melodious prayers punctuated by beatings on a handheld gourd. At the end of each passage, a gong was gently struck.

With a commanding voice, the master of ceremonies told us to come to the altar (we were on our feet now), and to bow to the portrait of Father. Through the haze, his portrait looked down at us (rather sternly, I thought). First a deep bow from the waist, then on our knees to bump our foreheads on the floor, kowtowing. We rose up to a standing position and repeated the ritual two more times. Dick performed first, then Harold. Then sister Doris and I paid our respects together. I was dreading seeing Father's coffin, but he had already been buried at the "Permanent Cemetery," high up on a hill in the southern part of the island, near the fishing village called Aberdeen.

The ongoing funeral services were divided into sevens, in weeks, and this was a big occasion as it was the seventh of the seven weeks. It had taken us forty-nine days to return home!

The family was not in the front reception room, but waiting for us in the privacy of the upstairs quarters. There was even laughter as our siblings thought we looked like pieces of charcoal. After one month of sailing on the SS *Katori Maru*, all four of us had sunburned our faces so that we were like pieces of crisp bacon. "Huk muk muk," said sixth sister Amy. "Black as ink." Ah Ma and Chieh gave thanks to Buddha that we had returned safely.

Everything seemed strange to me. Without realizing it, I had forgotten how to speak Chinese! It was awkward not to be able to come up with words that I needed. The first day, after my bath, I realized there was no towel, and we all had a good laugh when I pantomimed what I needed.

However, hearing only Chinese spoken and with so many siblings, I was soon chatting away with the others. Sixth sister Amy, just a few years old, delighted in enlarging my vocabulary. At night she and fourth sister Joyce and I all slept in Chieh's Chinese bed, which was enormous and almost square. Since there were no tucked-in sheets, we lay down whichever way we wanted, each with a separate covering. Chieh sang to us. If it was too warm to let the mosquito net down, she would chase the buzzing insects away with her large palm fan.

Officially, we were in mourning for three years. (In reality, it was just over two years. We have a way of counting the time to make it sound more filial.) We could wear no real jewelry, no real silk, only certain somber colors, mostly whites, blacks and blues. At the Diocesan Girls' School, one student asked me, "Are you very poor?" as Doris and I always dressed in blue cotton clothes. At that time, the students did not wear uniforms.

After Father died, we owed huge sums of money to the Hong Kong and Shanghai Banking Corp. Earnings from tenant properties in Wanchai, the Lee Theatre and Father's other businesses could barely pay the interest to the bank. Sister Doris, who lived with her mother Ah Ma, told me that every night Ah Ma shed tears.

Father had had good relations with the bank. After his sudden death and our dire predicament, his friend in the bank Arthur Morse, then the Chief Accountant, went out of his way to help our family. Eldest brother, Dick, and later Harold, returned home after finishing Oxford University and looked after the estate, with the other brothers joining as they grew up. To Sir Arthur Morse, later head of the Hong Kong Shanghai Bank, we owe a great debt of gratitude for his patience and belief in the integrity of the Lee family.

Ah Ma followed Father's wishes to level the whole of Jardine Hill. It was not until years later that Lee Hysan Estate Co., Ltd., as our family business is called, was able to build on this large property. The main street is Hysan Avenue, and satellite streets branch out with names of our villages in China. We developed modern office buildings which are now owned by a public company, The Hysan Development Co., which the family started years ago. It was ably run by our second brother's eldest son, H. C. Lee, and later by our fifth brother Wing Kit's son, Peter T. C. Lee. Father had hit the jackpot when he bought in the area of Causeway Bay. He would be proud of what his sons and grandsons have achieved with his dreams.

Doris and I returned to the Diocesan Girls' School on the Kowloon Peninsula. The short ride on the Star Ferry played quite a part in the lives of the teenage students, since the Diocesan Boys' School was in Kowloon, too. We never talked to the boys and pretended they did not exist.

I found the curriculum much to my liking. Mrs. Thomas taught us English composition and art, both favorite subjects. She was an excellent teacher, and I loved her. She tried to start something unheard of in Hong Kong: to get the teenage boys from the Diocesan Boys' School to give a dance party. I attended it, but the whole thing was a flop as we were all so shy. I was "keen" on petite Miss Lee, a Canadian-Chinese gym teacher who urged me to study Physical Education in Canada.

The final exams took place at the Hong Kong University. The huge hall was unfamiliar and intimidating. I studied hard at math, my weak subject. Since it was taught by the only male in the school, who was also my piano teacher, I did my best to please him. Finally, in my last year, I was top of my class.

DIOCESAN GIRLS' SCHOOL
KOWLOON

REPORT FOR *Summer* TERM *1931*

NAME *Ansie Lee* CLASS *I*

NO. IN CLASS *15* POSITION IN CLASS *1st*

Subject	Marks Gained in Exam.	Remarks	
Scripture	63	*Very good indeed.*	*M. C. B*
	94	*Shows interest*	
Grammar	83	*Very good indeed.*	*M. C. I.*
Composition	80	*Shows real ability*	*M. C. I*
Literature	82	*Excellent.*	*M. C.*
Dictation	82	*Very good.*	*M. C. I*
History	64	*Shall do good work.*	*W.W.*
Geography	81	*Very good indeed.*	*M.M.*
Reading *Drawing*		*Excellent*	*M.M.*
Domestic Science	72	*Very good.*	*M. C. I*
Arithmetic	81		
Algebra	58	*A good worker. Shows an*	
Geometry	62	*intelligent interest and should*	
Drawing *Trigonometry*	41	*do well, with care*	
Needlework			
Music			
French	36	*Careful work.*	*A.K.H.*

CONDUCT *Most interested, and makes an effort to please.*

FORM MISTRESS *M. C. Bedford*

9/ HEAD MISTRESS *E. K. Walters.*   [*Very good indeed*

NEW TERM BEGINS *September 15th*

A month's notice in writing is required before the removal of a pupil, otherwise a month's fees are due.

Ansie's DGS report card 1931 – ranked first in the class

Senior class at Diocesan Girls' School
Hong Kong c. 1931

Front row, from left: unknown, Ida Ng (Kan), Ansie (with glasses),
Ivy Kan (Fung), rest unknown
Back row, from left: Helen Ho, Helen Kotewall (Zimmern), Stella Ho
(Davreux), rest unknown

We never went anywhere during the long summer holidays, but instead had to create our own entertainment. I made up little plays in English, and Joyce, Amy and fifth sister Dione would perform them. For an audience we made brother J.S. sit and watch, but promised him something special for tea. Often that something special was a lemon meringue pie that we bought in town, walking down those long flights of steps to Queen's Road and taking a bus to the Canadian Café, then at the edge of the Central district.

I expect few of the younger siblings remember how hard up we were, but there was always "face" to be upheld, and the public was unaware of our predicament. Once when Doris and I were asked to a special party, she declined, stopping my pleas with, "What do you think we are going to wear?" To this day I remember her words and marvel at how unaware I was of our plight. A few years later when we were grown up, Wing Kit, our fifth brother, would drive us to a beach on the south side of the island, and coming home he would turn off the engine at the top of the hill to save petrol.

None of my DGS classmates went to college. I did not consider it, as Doris was not planning to go anywhere. Besides, we were living in an era when a high school education was enough if you were British and female. No one as yet had shown the way to go to the U.S. for their higher education. But it did happen a few years later, and many of our large family chose the U.S. for their college education.

Doris and I wanted to study Chinese, so with our friends from DGS, Ivy Kan, Helen Kotewall and Doris Kotewall, we entered Yu Sook Man's school. He had the only school that welcomed students of any age. Teacher Yu loved to expound the classics in his large one-room school.

I can picture him now, with his eyes half-closed, a book in one hand and a fan in the other, dressed in a long gray gown with cloth shoes. He was medium height, heavy-set and had lusty lungs so everyone could hear every word. He especially enjoyed the romantic passages, and we teenagers would look at each other and stifle giggles as he tried to explain these passages in colloquial terms.

One day on my way to the Chinese school I passed the Italian Convent School on Caine Road. At the gate there was a notice of shorthand and typing lessons given by a Miss Nunis. I went in and joined. That really changed my life. It was intriguing to be able to write "thank you for your letter" in just two curves. I didn't think typing would be much use. How wrong can one be!

I could not find anything to do, and soon I felt very depressed. Living in Hong Kong seemed like being in a pit, and I could not climb out of it. Brother Harold could see something was very wrong and took me to a doctor who, bless his heart, said I needed a change and should go away somewhere.

In the autumn of 1935 I went to Peking. It was an enchanting city. I stayed with the Hsiung family, anglicized to "Young." Auntie Young was related to my eldest sister-in-law, Esther, Dick's wife. Mr. Young was in the diplomatic service and was in South America.

There were three children still living at home. Didi was a good-natured chubby little brother, always with a grin on his face. Maizie, full of enthusiasm and fun, attended the Peking American School. Christine was two years my senior. Eddie, the eldest, was away studying medicine at the Peking Union Medical College (PUMC). He often came home for dinner bringing me packets of yeast powder for Vitamin B to put in my evening soup. From those early years, I have been a great believer in vitamins for better health.

Auntie Young was frequently invited to dinners with friends from the British and American diplomatic corps, and Christine and I were often included. I think the best cooks in China, for French, Russian and Italian dishes, were in those legations. There was an outstanding dessert called Peking Dust, fluffy chestnuts folded in whipped cream, held together with ladyfingers. This was topped with glazed fruit nestling in sculptured cream, and crowned with golden spun sugar. The chestnuts were never gooey, but fluffy.

Dinner party at British Embassy, Peking 1936
Ansie back row, right

While I was in Peking, I had lessons in Mandarin every day with Auntie Young's mother, who we called Grandma. I learned to speak Peking dialect with a pronounced burr in every sentence, and with a dictionary could write letters to my mother. My handwriting was better than expected as Doris and I had handed in pages of Chinese calligraphy each evening to J.S.'s tutor who used to come to our Hong Kong home in the earlier years.

Cantonese is fine for speaking since I cannot imagine another language that is so descriptive (and so earthy), but many of the spoken words are slang and have no written characters. A northern Chinese and a Cantonese cannot talk to one another using their own dialects.

Brother J.S. and Ansie, Peking 1936

In Mandarin, "Wing Sum" is "Jung Sen," so my fourth brother is known as J.S. He was a student at Yenching University, just outside Peking. How lucky I was to be in Peking at that time, 1935 to 1936, when I was just twenty-one. With college friends of J.S.'s, we had plenty of escorts and jolly groups for picnics and hikes on the Great Wall and dancing at the Grand Hotel des Wagon-Lits.

The Temple of Heaven was a rickshaw ride away from Ta Fang Jieh Hutung where the Youngs lived, but it took a strong runner to haul one of us that distance. Part of the magic of this loveliest of lovely places in China was the stillness there. At the Altar of Heaven you could whisper a message and the sound was sent around the marble wall to a friend listening on the far side.

There is no covering to this vast altar, as it is the center of the Universe and Heaven itself is the roof. Emperors made their sacrifices here, interceding for their people. The Temple of Heaven was farther on, encircled by white marble steps, with brilliant blue tiles on the roof, and scarlet pillars.

Ansie at the Temple of Heaven, Peking 1936

Returning home from these outings, we would stop near the city walls to eat Peking duck at our favorite restaurant. Inside the entrance was a funnel-shaped barbecue with several ducks hanging high above smoldering charcoal. The sudden warmth, the aroma of the juice and fat dripping onto the fire and the loud welcome by the owner were truly heartwarming. We would follow the beaming host upstairs and be given hot towels to wipe our hands.

The duck, puffed up and glistening a deep bronze, was proudly presented by the carver. Wielding a large chopper, he deftly sliced slivers of the crisp skin, then the meat. On the round dining table were dishes of bean sauce and whites of leeks sliced fine and cut about three inches long. Thin, warm, pliant wheat pancakes were offered. We placed a piece or two of the duck and leek and a dab of sauce onto the pancake. Rolling them up, we ate them, marveling at the crunch of the skin and the juiciness of the meat.

There were more dishes coming from the duck: savory custards, duck feet stewed in a rich brown gravy circled by bright mustard greens, and sliced livers and gizzards with their edges snipped as if by pinking shears. In the middle of the meal, a large bowl of bubbling soup made from duck bones and Tientsin cabbage was set on the table. (Of course, it was not made from our duck bones as the soup took hours of simmering.)

Northerners are wheat-eaters rather then rice-eaters. So we had warm "silver-threaded" buns, with the dough encasing a bundle of threads of the same dough. This pleased the eye and to a southerner like me, was an added delight. Then came the noodles, sautéed with the rest of the duck meat, greens, and finely sliced bamboo shoots and mushrooms.

We always had room for "toffee apples," pieces of hot fruit covered with a coating of candied sugar that were everyone's favorite ending to this Peking duck feast. When we rose to leave, we would hear a shout. The staff quickly lined up near the front door, bowing and calling, "Hsieh, hsieh" (thank you).

During the winter, we sometimes gathered around smoldering pine logs at the Mongolian food stall to barbecue paper-thin slices of mutton. This was my introduction to sixteen-inch-long wooden chopsticks used for turning the meat on the round dome-shaped grill. The marinade from the meat dripped onto the ashen hot logs, and they answered back by sizzling, spitting and sending up wisps of smoke and heavenly smells. In perhaps five seconds, you turned the meat on the grill to sear the other side and then stuffed the hot meat inside a sesame bun. Then you joined your friends around an outdoor table laid with plates of scallions and sauces and mugs of hot tea or small shots of *bai gar* (white lightning), a white innocent-looking liquid that is pure alcohol and can make your hair curl.

The EAT MORE CLUB! Would anyone these days want to belong to such a club? The gathering consisted of me and the three daughters of the US Military Attaché (later four-star General), Col. Joseph Stilwell[9]: Nancy, Winifred, known as Doot, and Alison.

The club also included the Young sisters, Christine and Maizie and another friend, Olive Wu. Doot and I became fast friends and

---

[9] World War II army officer, who headed both U.S. and Chinese Nationalist resistance to the Japanese advance on the Far Eastern mainland.

A 1904 graduate of the U.S. Military Academy in West Point, New York, Stilwell rose to the rank of general in 1944, having served in the Philippines, with the American Expeditionary Force in Europe during World War I, and as an instructor at West Point. In addition, he studied the Chinese language and later served in Tianjin (1926-29) and as a military attaché in Beijing (1935-39).

At the outbreak of World War II, Stilwell became General Chiang Kai-shek's chief of staff, and he was placed in command of the Chinese 5th and 6th armies in Burma (Myanmar). In 1942 he was routed by Japanese troops—superior in numbers and equipment—and arrived in India on foot with the remains of his command after an agonizing 140-mile (225-km) jungle trek. Through the war he served as commanding general of all U.S. forces in China, Burma, and India, and early in 1945 the Ledo Road, an Allied supply route linked to the Burma Road, was renamed the Stilwell Road in his honour. He was appointed commander of the U.S. 10th Army in the Pacific theatre, and in August 1945 he received the surrender of more than 100,000 Japanese troops in the Ryuku Islands.

After March 1946 Stilwell served as 6th Army commander in San Francisco until his death. "Joseph W. Stilwell." Encyclopaedia Britannica Online. 25 Jan. 2009 http://www.britannica.com/EBchecked/topic/566373/Joseph-W-Stilwell.

Col. Stilwell said I could call him "Pappy" as I was so much like Doot in temperament.

Col. Joseph P. Stilwell, U.S. Military Attaché
Peking 1936

At the Eat More club we exchanged recipes and did some cooking, played silly games and had much fun. It was especially nice when Olive Wu's chef taught us favorite dishes. I still have the worn-out Eat More Club recipe book.

The Eat More club members went to each others' homes, all nestled in narrow streets called *hutungs*, which formed a labyrinth

The Eat More Club, Peking 1936
Front row, from left: Christine Young, Maizie Young, Ansie
Back row, from left: Winifred Stilwell, Laura Ts'ao, Nancy Stilwell,
Olive Wu, Alison Stilwell

with no view of neighbors, only high walls and tops of trees. The hutungs led out onto the wide straight avenues surrounding the Forbidden City in the center of Peking.

Much to my surprise, as rickshaw-pullers rounded the blind corners of the narrow hutungs, they would shout warnings such as "borrowing light" or "facing north," or east, etc. They were so polite, not a bit like our southern coolies who peppered their sentences with swear words. The whole city was planned with horizontal and vertical streets so that you always knew in what direction you were going.

The Youngs' house in a Peking hutung

In the city, entire streets sold only silverware, others only jade, others brass, etc. The main shopping for everything was done at the Eastern Peace Market and visitors looked for wonderful "junk" jewelry Nowadays, these bracelets and earrings are highly regarded as they were made of silver and semi-precious stones. If you liked clocks, this market had many for sale. The Empress Dowager was known to like clocks, so foreign countries would present her with timepieces of every size and shape, many beautiful.

There was also the salesman who came to our house with linens, embroideries, curios and antiques. He displayed his wares on the living room floor and described to you what treasures he had found since his last visit, while sending fumes of garlic into the room.

Here in Peking I thought the time had come for me to be baptized and confirmed into the Church of England. Father had written to me in England that it would be fine if I wanted to become a Christian, but that it would be best if I waited a few years. Now, away from home, I went to Miss Mitchell, a missionary who ran a small place of worship in a lovely home in a hutung. The Bishop of North China came to conduct the service. One other candidate had also prepared for this important ceremony, an English soldier. Miss Mitchell said, "What kind of name is Ansie? Not a Christian name. You will be baptized Ansie Ann."

After a year in Peking, on July 4, 1936, J.S. and I returned to Hong Kong.

I thought I should find a job, but Brother Harold said he was not going to help me, and that I should not be working. Then what should I do? His answer really surprised me: Stay home and play the piano. It wasn't so outlandish at that time; I suppose "upper class" females did not go out to earn money. But I really needed some pocket money. Besides, I only enjoyed playing the piano when Doris played the violin.

I was already doing volunteer work, and by chance it was always connected with medical work. At Dr. Woo Wai Tak's clinics (he took out my appendix soon after I left school), I helped the office nurses take care of the wretched-looking opium addicts who came to his office once a week for treatment. ("They are so dirty," said one nurse, giving a little shudder.) Something was put on the back of a patient to create a large blister and the next week he would return to the doctor's office. My job was to draw the liquid out. Dr. Woo's assistant, a young Macao Portuguese, would inject the liquid back into the patient's arm. This was the cure, but did it work?

Most of the doctors in Hong Kong did pro bono work one morning a week. I was an assistant to Dr. Harry Talbot, an English doctor who helped at the Italian Convent hospital in Wanchai. He was a surgeon, and I translated for him as he walked through the ward. One day, however, I was suddenly thrust into a frightening job. I was in the operating room with a patient on the table all ready for the removal of something from his abdomen. Dr. Talbot was all scrubbed up. "I have to go," the Italian Sister said to me. "Will you please take over?" She left before I could reply. She had been about to give the patient chloroform. "Go ahead," Dr. Talbot said. "I will tell you what to do." It was not funny when the doctor asked me through his mask, "Is he dead yet?" A whole pan of foul-smelling liquid was scooped out of his innards. Fortunately, the patient lived.

My immediate family, Chieh, my two sisters Joyce and Amy and I, moved out of the Big House into the Lee Building, the large apartment building at the top of the garden. There were three enormous front rooms facing the harbor with high ceilings, and one small bedroom, just for me. We had a cat and a dog. Unlike most Chinese, Chieh liked animals. When an English friend gave me a spaniel, Peter, she let me keep him.

Doris asked me to be her bridesmaid at her wedding in September, 1937. It was a traditional Chinese ceremony where she and her husband, Kenneth Cheang, kowtowed to the ancestors.

Doris' wedding, Ansie as bridesmaid
Hong Kong, 1937

Brother Harold took me to our first cocktail party, on the British Flagship, the HMS *Tamar*. Officers danced with us, and I brightly asked my partner to what ship he belonged. There was a pause, and he said, "Let me see, I suppose I belong to all of them." At this point, a trim young man tapped him on the shoulder, and I was swept off to glide with my new partner around the deck under the stars. It was not until we said our thanks and farewells that I realized I had asked our host, the Commodore of the Fleet, that silly question.

I danced almost every night at Gripps, the dining room at the Hong Kong Hotel with charming young men who were properly introduced. It was almost like going to one's club. We often waved to the chef, Gaddi (later the famed chef at the Peninsula Hotel), if we happened to see him popping his head out from the kitchen to see who was enjoying his great dinners. Then, at the last stroke of midnight, we sang to the Filipino band's "God Save the Queen," properly restrained so as not to sound too jazzed up.

To return home by the upper road, Kennedy Road, one had to obtain a pass because a part of Kennedy Road ran above government property where the army explosives were stored. So our escort had to drive us home through Wanchai. Well, at midnight in Wanchai, "honey-carts" came to collect the toilet wastes to be used as fertilizer, known as night soil. Phew!

One of the young men I went out with often was Michael Walters, a British Naval officer stationed at a submarine base in Hong Kong. One day he took me to the base and we boarded a submarine, something that was strictly forbidden to visitors.

For more exercise I played tennis with J.S. and his classmates at home. I learned to hit hard as the opposition was all male. I went on launch picnics where I always felt seasick, and, naturally, miserable. I worshipped at St. John's Cathedral. But there was something missing. There was no real challenge. I needed to break out of this small island.

The Lee sisters in the garden of Dai Uk c. 1937

Front row, from left: seventh sister Diana and eighth sister Vivien
Back row, from left: fifth sister Dione, sixth sister Amy, Ansie
and fourth sister Joyce. Sister Doris had married.

CHAPTER 8
JAPAN'S WAR ON CHINA,
I LEAVE HOME: 1939

On July 7, 1937, one year and three days after I returned to Hong Kong from Peking, the newspapers reported an incident on the Marco Polo Bridge in North China where a Japanese soldier was shot and killed. The bridge was only a few miles southwest of Peking.

Col. Joseph Stilwell and his staff in the American Legation, the British, and other diplomats in Peking had a busy time keeping track of what was going on. The Japanese commander demanded that the supposed culprit, a Chinese soldier from the 29th Army, be handed over to him. Colonel Chi refused. Skirmishes followed and the Japanese took the nearby town of Wanping.

Four days after the Marco Polo Bridge shooting, Japan's Premier Prince Konoye ordered already poised troops totaling 150,000 men into China! Then came the demands: China was to hand over two of their northern provinces, Hopei and Chahar. This was the beginning of Japan's aggression toward China that lasted for eight more miserable years until the atomic bombs were dropped on Japan.

Japanese troops were well entrenched in China by the time the League of Nations adopted a resolution denouncing Japan's aggressive actions. Cordell Hull, the US Secretary of State, invoked the Kellogg-Briand Pact signed in 1928 by twenty-three nations including Japan, condemning "recourse to war for the solution of international controversies." But these were just gestures, and nothing came of them.

The Japanese army continued southward, controlling roads and railroads serving the cities. In just over a year, they occupied the whole length of the coastal regions and some central regions down to Canton, the capital of the southernmost province, Kwantung.

The head of the Chinese government, Generalissimo Chiang Kai-Shek, ordered his crack troops to defend Shanghai and Nanking, then the nation's capital. A few months later at the end of 1937, he was forced to retreat west to Chungking, in the far western province of Szechuan.

At the capture of Nanking, Japanese atrocities were photographed and filmed by observers, missionaries, Europeans, Americans and the Japanese themselves. These pictures were shown in nearby Shanghai where Henry Sperry, later to be my husband, was working at the time. Everyone was shocked at the unspeakable, bestial behavior of a "civilized" people.

By an inexplicable and unspoken "pact," the Japanese have been able for these many years to ignore their culpability to the Chinese, and in fact to the human race. This has been brought to the attention of the world by author Iris Chang in her graphic and well-documented book, the *Rape of Nanking*, published in 1997.

The bombing of Pearl Harbor in December of 1941 catapulted the United States of America into World War II, and this, painfully and slowly, turned the tide for China. China declared war on Japan, Germany and Italy. The United States helped the Chinese by sending war materiel and advisors to fight the Japanese. The spreading occupation of China finally ended on August 15, 1945, after the atom bombs were dropped on Hiroshima and Nagasaki.

My four years of schooling in England was at a very impressionable age, nine to thirteen years old. I had been completely submerged in the English way of life. There was no doubt in my mind that I had to "do my bit" for my country.

An Oxford classmate of my third brother, Harold, came from England to visit. John Leaning was good-looking and had a slight dent in the bridge of his nose from boxing, having been a boxing Blue at Oxford. (At Oxford and Cambridge, athletes are awarded the designation of "Blue" when they represent their school in a qualifying sport. Boxing is one of the oldest sports to have a received a Blue designation at both schools.) He took me to a meeting of The China Defence League, where they discussed the accomplishments of the Chinese communists at Yenan. I was much impressed.

John Leaning and Ansie 1938

Later I read in Ilona Ralf Sues's book, *Shark's Fins and Millet*, 1944, that the China Defence League had mobilized friendly democratic organizations all over the world. Mrs. Selwyn-Clarke was the honorary secretary. Her husband, Dr. Selwyn-Clarke, was the Medical Director of Hong Kong. Strongly supporting them was Madame Sun Yat-Sen, one of the Soong sisters. Whom did the China Defence League support? The criterion was serious, honest, democratic work. The International Peace Hospital in Wutaishan, the Yenan Base hospital, the Medical Service of the New Fourth Army, and Dr. Robert Lim's Training School stood at the head of the list. They were the nuclei of a permanent system of medical relief in China for the war years.

Early in 1939, a Chinese friend spoke to me about an Australian, W. H. Donald, who was advisor to Generalissimo Chiang Kai-Shek. She said to write to him about a job. I did so. Mr. Donald answered that they needed help in the Generalissimo's Headquarters in Chungking, but to wait until he returned from a trip to Madagascar. The sea trip was for his health. When he returned he tried to contact me, but by then I had already left for work with the Chinese Red Cross.

Another friend said she heard that the head of the Chinese Red Cross, Dr. Robert Lim, was in town and staying at the Hong Kong Hotel. I phoned Dr. Lim. He said he was just about to leave the hotel for lunch (he was in the main lobby when the receptionist handed him the telephone) and would be departing early next morning. (If I had phoned him a minute later, I may not have contacted him.) I would like to work for the Red Cross, I told him. He seemed pleased and after a very short conversation, he said he would leave a note for me at the hotel. I went the next morning to the hotel, and there it was. I still have the letter, hand-written on onion-skin paper on Hong Kong Hotel stationery.

March 4, 1939

Dear Miss Lee,

I am glad to know that you are willing to volunteer for services as a secretary at my H.Q. I am afraid the stipend is small ($60 National currency per month), but I believe you will find it adequate for living. There is ample work to do!

I suggest you proceed with Drs. Yik Wan and Talbot to Haiphong and come to Kweiyang by our trucks.

Please go to our Hong Kong office, should you decide definitely to come, and introduce yourself to the Sec.-General Dr. C. C. Pang, who will furnish you with the necessary papers.

Yours sincerely,

(Signed) Robert K. S. Lim

I was happy to see that I was to travel with Harry Talbot, for whom I had worked at the Italian Convent and of whom I had grown very fond. But I had no idea what to pack or what the weather was like, and none of my friends knew anything about Kweiyang, in Kweichow province. The name of the town meant "precious sunshine," and that should have given me a clue. The Red Cross office booked me on a French ship for Haiphong, in French Indochina. There were no Drs. Wan or Talbot on board.

My second brother saw me off, and he returned home really worried as he thought the steamer looked like a toy. Chieh never once disapproved of my plans, and if she had qualms for my safety, she did not show it. She had great faith in Buddha, God of Mercy. All her life she prayed three times a day, lighting incense and reading her book of prayers. Even when she was nearly a hundred years old she continued to pray, only instead of kneeling, she sat in an old rattan chair after we persuaded her that the gods would rather have her comfortable. Whenever her children returned home from their travels, her first act was to present extra food at the altar to express her thanks to her Gods.

On board this little miniature steamer, a big-boned Russian woman shared my cabin. I found out later she was a well-known communist, and so was her Chinese husband. That would not have bothered me, since the concept that everyone should share the wealth sounded fair. It never occurred to me that it might be that everyone shared the poverty. I was told later that those in power had endless perks.

On the little French vessel there were only four first class passengers. We ate dinner at a long narrow table with the French Captain and one or two other officers. Coffee was served and I lit my cigarette in its long holder. The Captain asked me which hotel would I be staying in. Hotel? I had not given it a single thought, and neither had the Russian woman.

"The port of Haiphong," said the Captain, "is teeming with people. *C'est la guerre.*"

"You won't find any rooms anywhere," said a middle-aged man, the manager of a Chinese bank. "I know, I am stationed there."

The steamer began rocking. The coffee had a strong, bitter chicory taste, made greasy with condensed milk. I never could drink even green tea with its caffeine, so this coffee was beyond my sphere, as it were. I never liked smoking. The lights were dim, the room hazy. I hoped no one noticed that I was slowly turning green.

The Russian lady and I went below to our cabin. It was hot and the cabin boy had left the portholes open. As we entered, the ship lurched to one side and, righting itself, gallons of seawater sloshed into the room. This not only frightened us, but also catapulted a big hairy spider across the cabin. My buxom cabin-mate gave a shriek, jumped onto her bunk and covered her head with the sheet. Really, I was more surprised by her actions than anything else.

"I am not going to sleep with that creature lurking around," I thought referring, of course, to the spider that had climbed up the cabin wall.

Squashing a spider, and such an enormous one, was revolting. The simple thing to do was, of course, yell for my amah. With a sinking feeling and realizing I was now in the big, big world alone, I did what my amah would do. With my shoe in hand and hoping the spider would not hear my thumping heart, I circled the shoe round and round above its head. Was it mesmerized? WHAM! The creature crumpled up into a ball and fell.

I had watched the amah go through this ritual with small spiders, and I was really quaking that this brute might shut its eyes. (I have never checked whether the eyes are on the top of their heads.)

The next morning at breakfast, the Chinese banker offered his apartment in his bank building in Haiphong for us. He had only one enormous bed, so I had to share it with the Russian. I never saw our kind banker again. It was only for one night as I was able to contact my group. Thank you so much, Mr. Banker.

The eight trucks donated to the Red Cross from Malaya along with volunteer drivers were waiting in Haiphong to proceed to Kweiyang, China. Also waiting was Harry Talbot, who was leading this convoy. The drivers spoke only Malay and English. Harry spoke no Chinese, so I was the sole interpreter. I was put into a responsible position right from the start, which was not my normal choice as I had always had my sister Doris to lean on.

It would have been comical if Cantonese were my only dialect as our route went through provinces where my native tongue was incomprehensible, but everyone seemed to understand Mandarin. Thank heavens I shared Grandma Young's teacher during my visit to Peking.

In Vietnam, only Vietnamese drivers were allowed to drive to the Chinese border, and we had to wait until nightfall. There is a mountain range between the two countries. It was spring. The roads were muddy, and we were constantly making sharp turns, snaking up and down the mountains. We saw a vehicle at the bottom of a ravine.

Finally at dawn we reached the Chinese border town of Dong Dang where our Malay drivers took over. But first, we stopped for breakfast at a food stall. We ate standing up; there were no tables or chairs. I had four fried eggs with French bread, and a large brimming mug of hot coffee with sweet condensed milk. I was surprised at the smallness of the eggs, all four yolks nestled together with their shiny faces and a crisp golden collar that looked the size of the palm of my hand. I ordered another plateful, polished that off and yet another. I shall always remember my "petit dejeuner" with twelve eggs in that hazy dawn on the edge of China.

We drove in a northerly direction without a hitch until we came to a small river where there was to be a ferry. There was no one there, so we yelled and tooted until a man came out of a hut on the opposite bank. Harry Talbot told me to fill my lungs and shout to him that these trucks were for Madame Chiang Kai-Shek, rather than the Red Cross, to impress him. The ferryman came over at once in a sampan carrying stout lines that were fastened onto some pilings. Following his directions, the trucks, a few at a time, were loaded onto a flat barge and pulled over to the other side.

By the time we arrived at Nanning in Kwangsi province, night had already fallen. We knocked on the door of the Mission Hospital run by Dr. Coffin, an American, and were received with smiling faces. We had medical supplies for them.

To our dismay our convoy had to return to Haiphong the next day to pick up more medical supplies, so the trip was repeated. Although the law stated only Vietnamese were allowed to drive over this range, on our second trip through the mountains the Vietnamese driver was so overworked and tired that he begged Dr. Talbot to drive as he was falling asleep! The road was the same, but now we knew what we were up against. It did not make it any less fearful. Trucks larger than ours could not make the U-turns on many of the steep mountain roads. They had to stop, and with the engine roaring, reverse and try again. We completed the journey to the medical mission, and after a good night's sleep we finally started to head north through the length of Kwangsi Province into the neighboring province of Kweichow.

Little did I realize that sleeping on a bed at the hospital was the height of luxury. We didn't have a roof over our heads for the rest of the trip, but at least I had a stretcher taken out of a truck and placed under a tree.

There is much to wonder at in this world, but nothing ever compared to the astonishment I felt as we drove through Kwangsi Province. We came upon a scene straight out of Grimm's Fairy Tales. Stretching before us was a line of skinny jagged peaks, packed close together and resembling humans with waving arms. As we approached, we saw they were made of stunted trees growing from the steep sides of pointed mounds. We drove on flat ground, twisting and turning as we threaded through the breadth of this limestone range. Shafts of the setting sun pierced the spaces to create a truly surreal scene.

Heading in a northwesterly direction, we now had to change our plans and only drive at night, as the Japanese had occupied towns to the east of us. Their warplanes would come swooping down, strafing any motor transport they spotted. Our convoy stayed under cover from dawn to dusk. We heard the drone of their planes and the thud of bombs as they went on their missions. Luckily, we escaped detection and arrived at the Chinese Medical Relief Corps in Tuyunkwan above the city of Kweiyang, on April 4, 1939, exactly one month from the day I had applied for the job.

CHAPTER 9
MEDICAL RELIEF CORPS,
KWEIYANG: 1939

What a surprise! The organization I was working for was not the Chinese Red Cross, but the Medical Relief Corps. The MRC was set up in 1938 in Hankow by a group of dedicated professionals, who, for love of their country, formed the nucleus of medical help for the Chinese army. It was a civilian organization funded by a wealthy Chinese man from Shanghai and was under the auspices of the Chinese Red Cross. However, the MRC's funds also came from donations from charitable and private sources.

With the advance of the Japanese occupation of China, the MRC moved from Hankow westward to a secluded mountain pass, Tuyunkwan, above the city of Kweiyang in Kweichow province.

Dr. Robert K. S. Lim, Professor at the Peking Union Medical College (PUMC), headed this wonderful organization. His field was physiology, and he was the youngest doctor ever to be appointed a Professor at the PUMC, which was established by the Rockefeller Foundation. Other doctors from the PUMC, as well as nursing staff, joined him. He recruited Chinese and foreign doctors trained in different parts of the world.

I had no idea what kind of environment I had thrown myself into. The grounds of the MRC lay sprawled on both sides of a cleft in a mountain pass. The long, barn-like buildings were made of wood with mat walls and thatched roofs with stamped-down earth floors.

Medical Relief Corps headquarters 1939
Tuyunkwan, near Kweiyang
Kweichow Province, China

When I arrived, there was no electricity in the dorms. Faucets were outside our building. The toilet facility for our barracks consisted of an ingenious use of a diverted mountain stream over which was built an enclosed platform, looking like another building. It had cubicles and holes on the floor, which was hosed down daily. Outside this "loo," the stream ran underground.

Mud paths connected the dorms, classrooms, workshops, motor sheds, storeroom, and a few cottages. Ditches flanked the main paths. That spring of 1939 there was no outside lighting. I can still remember how afraid I was going home after working late. I had to thread my way gingerly down the slope, across the main road and up to the other side. How grateful I was when the moon showed the way and the stars were not just for gazing, but were my friends. My Hong Kong leather shoes leaked, and soon I had to pad them with folded up newspapers. It hardly helped. Fortunately, I never once slipped into the deep gutters.

Almost immediately I made a new friend, Joan Wang. We worked at the same long table in the General Office with a typewriter in front of each of us. There was also a Mr. Wong, a cheerful, young clerk at the office.

Joan Wang was the only other female office worker. She had joined the MRC before they moved here and so she knew everyone. Her father was Chinese, a professor at a university in Shensi province. Her mother was English. I liked Joan right away. She had a round face with a sweet smile and was usually full of exuberance, bursting into familiar English songs at surprising moments. We were the same age. She was taller than my 5'2" and had long, shiny dark brown hair brushed in various ways. She lent a touch of softness to the otherwise stark surroundings.

Later, when I heard she was a great tennis player, my admiration increased. A few years earlier, when her mother had taken Joan and her sister Winifred to Manila to compete in the Asian Games, the other contestants were amused at the two country bumpkins from some interior Chinese province—Shensi? They wore old tennis frocks, and who was their coach? No coach? Why yes, their Mum was their coach. The smirks of the other contestants turned to embarrassment when Joan beat them to become champion, not just for one year but several times. And playing with her sister Winifred, she won the doubles as well.

Joan Wang, a volunteer doctor and Ansie
Tuyunkwan, Kweiyang 1939

At the MRC, all correspondence was in English. Dr. Lim spoke Mandarin, but could not read Chinese. He had grown up in Singapore and studied medicine in Edinburgh.

Joan translated the Chinese reports that came from the Red Cross units stationed with the army. My first job was to rewrite the English ones as they were often hard to decipher, being scribbled in pencil, crumpled up or phrased in fractured English so that it would take too much time for Dr. Lim to read them.

One day while I was at the General Office typing, Chief (as Dr. Lim was called) came in and he and I chatted for the first time. When he found out that I could take shorthand he transferred me to his own office further up the hill, and I became his secretary.

Chief took me along when he visited the nearby field hospital and gave talks in English, which I took down in shorthand. Another Chinese doctor would translate his talks into Chinese. He was a great leader, very strict. He ran this huge establishment with a firm hand and was respected by all the staff. I found him always to be full of good humor and kindness, which made life pleasant.

Dr. Robert K.S. Lim ("Chief")

From my diary:

17th April, 1939. Wrote a letter for Chief today to International Red Cross asking for help for New Fourth Army. Japs started big offensive to wipe them out. Very pleased my first letter O.K.'d. It is pitiful to see these pathetic begging letters from the boys at the front lines. They want so little—not enough covering for the wounded so they want pillow cases, blankets etc. Money from just one big dinner party in Hong Kong would be enough to buy everything they ask for.

It seemed that every day it rained, and the thatched roof did only a fair job with leaks, so keeping our beds dry was frustrating. We draped them with plastic sheets and opened our umbrellas over our pillows. Joan and I improved our home by putting up a few pictures and by elevating my trunk between our cots so that we could put our oil lamp there. Later that year we had electricity.

Rats would eat whatever food we had, so there were tins and bottles for everything. These were placed on shelves. When I was sick for several days and stayed in bed, I met the king rat. He was the biggest rat I have ever seen. At nine o'clock sharp, he ambled across the room as he did each morning, expecting me to be away. I forgot to mention that Kweiyang was famous for its rat population.

From my diary:

5th May, 1939. What a commotion there was this evening! At 9 p.m. the rain suddenly started, coming down in torrents. Thunder and lightning, too. I was at the General Office, and everyone had to huddle in the central part of the building. Within five minutes, the paper ceiling was drenched and flopped down in patches, hanging like rags. The ground was inches in water, and the typewriters, which I had carefully placed under the table but elevated, were pretty damp.

Went up to the dorm, and there was Joan, perched on the edge of her camp bed, holding an umbrella and reading Disraeli *near the oil lamp. The whole room was flooded. Luckily our beds were dry due to having oilcloth placed on them. Dr.* Tu Kai-Yuan [a returned German medical graduate] *was our Sir Galahad. He came up to our barracks to see how we were faring and without saying another word, found shovel and bucket and, wearing high galoshes, scooped out as much water as he could from our room. Such gallantry; Joan and I love him for it. I hear the rat again.*

Sunday, 6ᵗʰ May, 1939. What a wonderful day this has been! Sunny again and clear. I put on a blue woolen cheongsam [my dresses were always Chinese] *and my jacket of many colours and even wore a little make-up.*

Attended finishing exercises of about a hundred Training School students. Went into town with Joan who took me to have tea at the International Red Cross. Scones and BUTTER. Went shopping and had supper with Colonel Hsiao, Joan, Mr. Tsuai and Kai Yuan. Took a rickshaw and walked up the hill. Saw the farewell plays for this training school class. HEAPS of fun and wonderfully acted plays. Lasted from 7:30 p.m. to 11:45 p.m! Have walked so much that I feel tired.

My salary amounted to pocket money and a plate of food at lunchtime brought over to our office. I do not remember going to the dining hall. However, with a few doctors, Joan and I often walked up the main road to a roadside food stall and ordered simple but well-cooked dishes. Joan reminded me recently how we put our chopsticks in boiling water before using them.

Soon after I began working for Chief, he invited Joan and me to eat lunch with him daily. He had brought his own cook from Peking with him. Can you imagine such good fortune for us? I believe he missed his family and told me I reminded him of his daughter, Effie. He had a Scottish wife who had passed on a few years earlier.

I bought a grey cotton uniform for National Currency $4. It looked quite smart but after its first wash it became perpetually wrinkled. We used a hand basin to do our laundry and, on rare sunny days, hung our clothes on a line outside the building. Mostly we lit a charcoal stove in our tiny cubicle; it's a wonder we did not burn down the dorm or die of asphyxiation. I gave up trying to iron the uniform with a charcoal iron.

The constant spring rain brought a profusion of wildflowers. It was a joy to look across the valley and see shades of mauve, then, to our delight the Painter added sweeps of sunny yellows with his broad brush. Those times lifted our spirits.

Enclosed with a letter from Harry Talbot was an unattributed poem entitled "Flowers." He was on the road from Kweiyang down to Kweilin, returning to Hong Kong after having delivered the trucks we had driven from Hanoi to the Fourth Army. His letter was dated 28th April, 1939. There were dog roses, "wild and white and pure. Bridal sprays, that do not long endure. Vermilion azaleas adorn the blushing mountain sides." Heliotrope, the wood-oil and pear trees, lilies and "Lovely iris in profusion, cheer our way in purple splendour."

The Miaos, aborigines living in this area, added more color to the scene as they trekked on the main road, passing our sprawl of wooden structures. Their garb was nothing that I had ever seen before. The women adorned themselves with heavy silver necklaces, bangles on their arms and dangling earrings. They wore long, loose, brightly colored embroidered skirts and jackets, with no collars such as we Chinese have, woven on looms with traditional designs and strong colors. The men differed from the Chinese in that they always wore turbans.

A Miao woman

Dr. Lim gave Joan and me an assignment that made my heart skip a beat. We were to go to Kunming and pick up three German doctors who had been fighting in the Spanish civil war. They were offering their services to our Medical Relief Corps and were due to cross into China through Indochina.

Kunming is the capital of Yunnan, at the southwestern edge of China, touching Burma and Indochina. This mountainous province is crossed by three major rivers: the Yangtze, here in its upper reaches known as the Kinsha (Golden Sands), the Mekong and the Salween. All have carved great gorges.

What a thrill to see this fertile plateau of Kunming, bathed in crisp cool air at 6400 ft. Here, several aboriginal tribes lived: the Miaos, Lolos and Shans. This isolated part of the world remained unconquered during the development of China, and it was not until the 17th century that it capitulated and became part of China.

We waited for the doctors, but they did not appear. We waited in style, staying at a very grand hotel on an island in a big lake. Joan and I had baths (my first since arriving in China) and ate large juicy pomegranates, peaches and melons, and the famous Yunnan ham (similar to Virginia ham). We wondered at the large sooty handprints on the walls that enclosed the homes, and we visited historical spots. I even went horseback riding, the mare trying to toss me over her head, reminding me of my one and only hunt meet on the Sussex Downs in England. Only this time I stayed on.

Finally we heard our German volunteers had taken another route into China, and so we headed for home, filling our trucks with goods for our MRC.

From my diary:

26th July, 1939. Exciting day. Jim is here [Jim Bertram, a New Zealand journalist and Rhodes Scholar whom I had met several times in Hong Kong], *arrived 21st July in the evening with Corin Bernfeld and Dr. & Mrs. Kiang. There was most enlightening talk with three doctors from Spain* [the Germans that we had gone to Kunming to bring back]. *We were in Jim's room as he was in bed with a touch of fever. Talked of war, of course, in Spain and in China. Heard about concentration camps on French border, on seashore, no barracks, no food; they ate what they had brought themselves from Spain. Wish Jim could stay longer. A grand person.*

Least of all that happened was Joan and I had a raise; we now will get from 1st August, NC$80 per month. At the moment the exchange rate is HK$1 to NC$4. Corin left today for Chungking with our Hanchung group to start a branch of the Training School. Am reading Jim's North China Front. *Well written. He wrote a poem in my autograph album.*

Tuyunkwan, Kweiyang, 3ʳᵈ August, 1939. Jim left early this morning. We didn't see him off. He's going to Chungking. Have developed a passion for poetry and even try reading German ones.

I weigh 114 lbs. Am reading The Way of All Flesh. *Also read a bit of* North China Front, *Jim Bertram's book.*

Unconquered, the U.S. edition, is better.

Jim Bertram in Kweiyang 1939

My things from Home came about ten days ago. Shoes, uniform, toffee!

Sunday, 6ᵗʰ August, 1939. I have just gone through my first air-raid alarm in a city.

Not having been to town on a Sunday for over two months, I decided to take the whole day off from work and went with Joan to see her mother and sister, Winifred, who were staying at the Kweiyang Guest House. We had a very good Cantonese lunch and went back to the Guest House to keep Winifred company. Win looked very pale and had to rest as she had given birth to a baby boy. She did not go out to lunch with us as she was too weak to walk.

For the next few hours after lunch, we played records which were brought out specially for her and Mrs. Wang by Dr. T. S. Sze [now spelled Shi] who did all the winding, playing Beethoven's Symphony No.5 in C minor and Mendelssohn's Concerto in E minor. T.S.owned these records. We have listened to them countless times in his quarters at the Red Cross.

At 4:45 p.m., while I was talking to some Germans, also staying at the Guesthouse, the air-raid alarm was heard. It was rather faint, and only lasted a few minutes. A long and short sound, something between a foghorn and a siren. My first indication of the alarm was not the sound itself, for it was faint and, never having heard it before, I did not recognize the significance. Someone in the room shouted "AIR-RAID" and everyone jumped up. I knew at once we had to get out of the house. The first thought was to get Win and the baby downstairs.

People were milling around the courtyard gathering whatever they could carry. Someone in our group managed to hire a rickshaw. The whole atmosphere was tense with fear and urgency. My brain seemed to divide itself into two sections, one quite outside myself, thinking calmly 'now that it's happening I wonder how you will act. You had better not run, just walk.' Down in the courtyard one of the Germans was calling, "Hurry, Miss Wang, please hurry." Almost everyone had already left when slowly Joan and I, on each side of Win, bundled her and baby into the rickshaw.

The alleyways were already deserted with only two policemen on guard. Winding left and right we finally reached the wide streets. Here there were crowds of people, all headed in the same direction. Suddenly I felt a few drops of rain on my face. It cannot be, thought I, for only ten minutes before the sky was clear and full of sunshine. "It's raining," I shouted, and within a few minutes it was pouring.

Near the East Gate of the city's wall were hundreds of people, trying to get shelter under sheds and trees. We passed two air-raid dugouts on the side of the road, muddy looking holes with steps leading down. Uh! I'd hate to get into one of those.

After walking for half an hour, feeling thoroughly wet and muddy, we decided to stop on the side of the country road. We thought, with the rain, surely they can't come. "If the planes come," said Joan to me, "you must lie flat on the ground because they will try to machine-gun us." However, another German told us to move on. "It's very bad place to stop, you must get off the road." There were hundreds all around us. Some soldiers were among the crowd. A man with a cat passed us; the cat meowed, hating the rain.

As the city was infested with rats, a cat was worth saving!

A little tailor lugged his cumbersome sewing machine heavy with its foot pedal, looking grim but no doubt thankful he had wheels to haul his machine.

We finally came to a lane. On one side were two huts, and here we tried to get a little shelter. From the smell we knew we were sharing it with an ox. Another half-hour, then the all clear signal was heard. This time the siren was a continuous one.

Coming back, exhausted, the Red Cross truck broke down so we started to walk up the hill for home. The truck was fixed, picked us up and brought us home. I'm dead tired now; midnight.

7th August, 1939. Went up after dinner and chatted with Chief. Talked about the coming 4th Report. Chief likes smoking

Edgeworth tobacco but "will smoke cabbage leaves if there isn't anything else."

Win and Mrs. Wang moved out here and are sleeping with baby and the amah in a tent.

8th August, 1939. Mrs. Selwyn-Clarke arrived just before lunch, from Kunming. Chief's house still looks like a 'railway station' as he called it yesterday. Painters varnishing the woodwork, glass fitter for the windows, carpenters outside. I started making draft copy of the semi-annual report (4th) as soon as Chief finishes a page. As his office is being painted, we both work in the living room, with a screen between us!

9th August, 1939. All morning took notes of conversation between Chief and Mrs. Selwyn-Clarke. Had lunch and dinner with them at Chief's house, which is also his office. For dinner there was chicken, potato chips, tomatoes and a pudding. Also a wine which tasted like vermouth. They talked about birth control. Did we need it at the Red Cross, there being so many boys and girls, asks Mrs. S.C.?

10th August, 1939. Felt sick all day. However stuck through it. Mrs. Selwyn-Clarke leaving tomorrow so tried to get all she wanted to know together. Took a photo of her having tea with several people outside Chief's house. Lunched with Chief and Mrs. S.C.

7 p.m. Up in dorm going to bed. Reading Julian Huxley's 'Essays of a Biologist.'

11th August, 1939. Mrs. Selwyn-Clarke left at 11:10 a.m. Had sandwiches which Joan made (we lost our Mantou [a northern bun] *which was left overnight at the office.) At Chief's House Wm. Hu asked, "Why you eat all time?" Mrs. S.C. is a remarkable woman, and an absolute dear.*

Feel quite all right again today. Chief asked Fatty Yung and me to dinner. Very nice.

Tea party for Shanghai Unit in Chief's newly painted house.

15th August, 1939. We had a fish for lunch! Cost $2. The little restaurant must have bought it from a passing fisherman.

16th August, 1939. There was a wedding today in the city and saw many Red Crossers in civilian clothes. 'Mother T.F.' said he hadn't worn a suit for two years. In fact ever since he joined the Chinese Red Cross.

Wrote several letters and received one from Michael [Walters], *who is on his way from Hong Kong to Singapore, and then home to England.*

1st September, 1939. At 8 p.m. we heard the news over the radio from Manila that Germany had bombed seven cities in Poland, bombing Warsaw at 9 a.m. and then again an hour later. Is this the beginning of another world war?

France has enforced the Mobilization Act. London will attend Parliament later today, and two million school children are being immediately evacuated from London. Hitler made declarations to his people and has stated that if anything happened to him Goering and then Hess were to succeed him.

This morning about 10:30 a.m. there was an air-raid alarm. About half an hour later we heard the planes. 29 were over Nantau on the Kweichow border. Chief told us to leave the house. It looked very serious today. Joan, Miss Kung, [a teacher at the nursing school], *and I went up the mountain taking books and our jerseys that we had at the office. We thought at least we'd keep warm when night fell and our things had been bombed! It was boiling hot under the sun. I had my Indo-Chine straw hat.*

War, and the dread of war, all over the world. It is strange to be in the midst of one and to hear another war is to be started.

I traveled to Chungking with Chief when he went for meetings in September. While there I had a meeting with W.H. Donald.[10] He sent his car to pick me up at the hotel, and we talked for about half an hour at the Generalissimo's Headquarters. He told me to call him Don. All I knew about Don was that he was an advisor to China's Head of State, Generalissimo Chiang Kai-Shek. Don and I hit it off right away, and he asked me to come work for him in Chungking. Don must have been very persuasive for I was happy with all my friends at the Medical Relief Corps, especially as Chief was an inspirational boss and always had time to be thoughtful and kind to both Joan and me. For reasons I can only think of as fate, I told Don I would talk to Chief about my working in Chungking for my "war effort."

7ᵗʰ November, 1939. Wrote letter to Chief telling him I want to go to Chungking to work.

8ᵗʰ November, 1939. Chief understands and it is O.K.!! Without a talking to! I believe he must have heard from W.H. Donald.

---

[10] Donald, William Henry (1875-1946), was a foreign correspondent and adviser born in Lithgow, New South Wales. As a journalist in Hong Kong and Shanghai, he was at first a decorated admirer of Japan, but by 1915 had become a vocal critic. He became an advisor to Chiang Kai-shek, and mediated the Sian *coup d'etat* in 1936. After a disagreement over Chiang Kai-shek's policy towards Germany, he left China in 1940. After touring the Pacific in 1940-41, he was returning to China at Madam Chiang's request when he was captured in Manila in January, 1942. Throughout his imprisonment by the Japanese, first in the University of Santo Tomas Camp and in Los Baños, he managed to conceal his identity. Liberated in February, 1945 he returned to China in 1946, where he died in Shanghai that same year. *Australian Dictionary of Biography Online Edition.* Retrieved 1/1/09.

12th November, 1939. Sun Yat-Sen's birthday. Shall be leaving on the 18th by Red Cross truck with T.Y. Koo, the Sanitary Engineering boss.

13th November, 1939. Cold and wet. Always wearing my grey flannel pants these days. Went to the tailor to see about a jacket for the pants. Received a letter from Michael who just landed in England. I feel so sad when I hear from him.

I had received a telegram from Michael Walters this month asking me to marry him. I can't remember exactly how I answered him, but I said that it was not possible. We were always just good friends and were never committed in any way. He died soon after the war began, in a submarine or sunk by a submarine. I never found out until after the war.

Kweiyang, 17th November, 1939. Have been wanting to write and yet never finding the time, energy or this book (no more excuses Ansie). Was told by Dick Loo that we can't start tomorrow for Chungking after all.

On the 15th at dinner Chief expressed his feelings about my going. "I'll tell Donald he's taking away my only assistant." That statement was made emphatically, and after a few inarticulate moments, I replied I was honoured to be thought of as such. Then he added, "Look here, how about just loaning you to Madame Chiang to be our representative at the Generalissimo's Headquarters. You can quit without too much bother anytime you want. We'll take you back anytime you wish."

I did not know that once you work for Madame, you can never quit.

On the 14th, Dr. Chiang ('Mother T.F') gave me a farewell party. Everyone so friendly, our staff and two from the Medical Dept.

16th November, 1939. 'Blimey' [Dr. Wong a returned medical grad from England] *and Jensen,* [one of the German doctors] *(just returned from Hunan front) took Joan and me to dinner, also Eric Landauer, to the new restaurant up the hill at Tuyunkwan. These two days the lovely sun came out, and I took lots of photos, some of the fourteen Spanish doctors* [they were all Germans who had volunteered in Spain]. *How I shall miss the hills, the flowers and the strange life.*

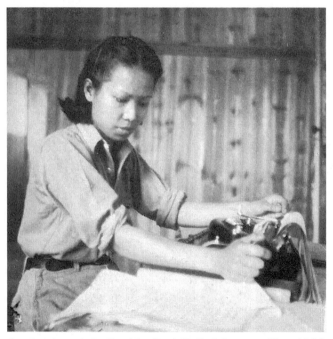

Ansie at work in the Medical Relief Corps office 1939

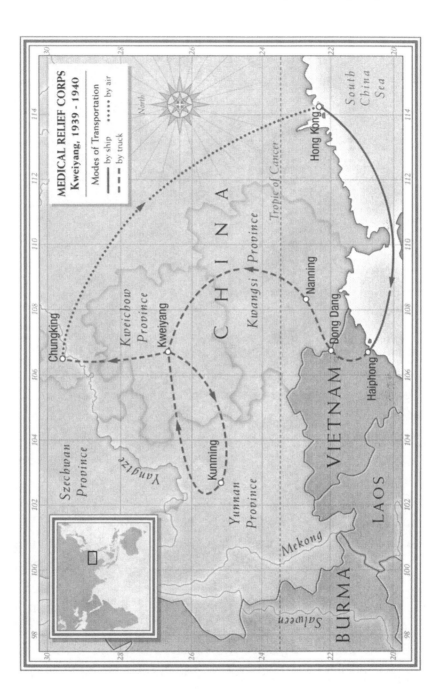

CHAPTER 10
CHUNGKING & W.H.DONALD:
1939-1940

On November 18, 1939, I left the Medical Relief Corps at Tuyunkwan and bade Chief, Joan, T.S. and the finest group of volunteers, farewell. Mr. T. Y. Koo, head of the Sanitary Engineering Department, and I climbed onto a Red Cross truck to Chungking. There I was met in town by W.H. Donald, and we were driven quite a distance to the Headquarters of Generalissimo Chiang Kai-Shek.

It was late and dark, and I could not see anything of the landscape. We drove through a gate with high walls and arrived at a large building. I was given a room on the second floor, right next to a large office where only one other young woman worked. Alas, she was not another Joan Wang, and in fact I had the feeling she did not want me there. "Cheer up. There's a war on," I said to myself.

I did not feel at all strange with W.H.D. There are some people you take to right away. He was always amusing and had a twinkle in his eye. Besides, he had bombarded me with telegrams full of jokes in code from Chungking for all those weeks before leaving Kweiyang, He had said at our first meeting in Chungking, "I'll keep in touch but it will be in code." It's a wonder that Chief did not haul me up to ask me what was going on. No doubt his mailing department had broken the code. It was a lot of fun and made me smile.

Madame and Generalissimo Chiang Kai-Shek with schoolchildren;
W.H. Donald in the background

Since I stopped keeping a diary, there are only a few episodes that stay clear in my memory. The most exciting one was going next door to take dictation from Madame Chiang. I went alone and walked through the small gate between the two large compounds. I believe they cut the wall especially for W.H.D., their Australian

Advisor. I was admitted to Generalissimo and Madame Chiang's house without any fuss. I smiled to the man standing guard at the bottom of the stairs and was quite startled to see a secret service chap at every turn in the stairway. I was ushered into Madame's boudoir.

Seated on an armchair was Madame Chiang, one of the three Soong sisters - Mei-Ling. I was familiar with her New Life Movement, which she designed, the press applauded, and all were told to heed and follow. I was so naive that I was taken aback by the beautiful lady who greeted me, arms extended to wave me onto a chair, with varnished pink nails, smoking a cigarette marked with red lipstick. She spoke with an American accent. We exchanged pleasantries. Her first letter was to the French Ambassador to thank him for some perfume. "Would you say it was 'delicious'," she queried?

It did occur to me what Madame must have thought of me, looking like, well, what her "New Life Movement" wanted me to look like; I was decidedly Plain Jane, wearing my old Red Cross clothes (I had little else), with a scrubbed face. The fatal blow to my self-esteem was when the "Gissimo" (that was what Don called him) came in to take his wife downstairs to dinner. I stood up and should have greeted him by saying, "Good Evening, Generalissimo Chiang," in plain English. Instead I made a frantic reach into my little brain to try to remember how to address him in Chinese. I was flushed with embarrassment as Madame took his arm and walked out.

I helped with Madame's personal correspondence. Don was always at the office, and there he rattled off his articles and personal letters on his typewriter. The other secretary did not show me where anything was and did her best to make me feel unwelcome. In fact, after one week she disappeared. There were many visitors, mostly VIPs like H.H. Kung, the Finance Minister, and Don's Chinese friends. I liked Hollington Tong who came frequently to visit Don. Emily Hahn—the author who came to Chungking to interview Madame for her book on the three sisters—was curious about me. She only saw me closing the door to my room, so all she could write about me was seeing my slacks disappearing from view.

I only went out once, to the Foreign Correspondents Club. There, as Don predicted, I was approached by Russians to teach them English. They would also ask me innocuous-seeming questions, such as, "What was Madame wearing today?" But Don told me later that what they really wanted to know was if she was in residence.

In my little world, supper was brought up to the office from the staff kitchen. It was always at 5 p.m. On clear days even before I could start eating, the air-raid alarm would sound. I would make a quick exit to a waiting car where I was driven to a very exclusive shelter where Madame went, and sometimes Don, but the Gissimo was busy elsewhere. Poor Chungking would be in flames, making an awesome display, always, thankfully, in the distance.

The Japanese strategy was to bomb the cities into submission. I read later that Chungking suffered 268 raids between May 3rd, 1938, and 1941, mostly during the summer months when the skies were clear. At that time it held the gruesome record of the most bombed city in the world. The people of Chungking survived. Their air-raid shelters were blasted out of the solid rock on which the city was built. They had ample time to gather their families to hide. The warning system for approaching enemy warplanes was alerted by secret Chinese radio contact near the enemy airfield.

I felt rather like a bird in a cage and my health suffered from lack of exercise, fresh air and social contacts. It wasn't long before

Ansie in the office in Chungking 1939

Don saw that although I never complained, life in Chungking was not for me. I became thinner and thinner until finally he put me on a flight back to Hong Kong.

When I recovered my health, Don came to Hong Kong with Madame Chiang. He met my sister Joyce and Chieh, my mother. They both liked him right away. He asked Joyce to call him "Gran." (Madame Chiang called him that.)

W.H. Donald in the office in Chungking 1939

Don wanted me to return to Chungking with him. In early April, 1940, I went on the historic flight back with the three Soong sisters: Ching-Ling, the wife of Sun Yat-Sen, Ai-Ling, the wife of H.H. Kung, and Mei-Ling. They had not been together for a long time. It was a large plane with just a handful of us. Besides Mesdames Sun, Kung and Chiang, there was a renowned Chinese lady advocate who had a robust voice that carried to the tail end of the plane where I quietly sat with a man from the HQ office. The plane took off from Hong Kong after dark, if you can imagine such a crazy way to go, with the dense buildings on one side and Lion Rock looming just ahead.

My second stay in Chungking was again short. I was happy to meet Don's friends, one of whom, McHugh, came almost daily. I was asked to join them on their walks on the large flat roof of the building. It was here that I learned that Don was longing to have his yacht in Hong Kong launched and to sail off on her to do some writing. He thought the sea off Indochina would be splendid, with its quaint little islets popping out of the blue waters of Baie Dalong. This, I thought, sounded just like the whipped up dollops of limestone peaks that we drove through in Kwangsi Province on my entry into China with the Red Cross trucks. By this time, my relationship with Don had deepened, and he didn't have to ask me to join him on the sailing adventure; we both knew that I would.

Don and I left the Generalissimo headquarters, and this time for good. If anyone has kept letters from Madame with "A.L." at the bottom of the page, those are my initials. As for Don, I heard him say to friends, "Do not call me Advisor as no one takes my advice." He meant, I suppose, that Chiang Kai-Shek was more interested in his German advisor's interpretation of the war in Europe.

CHAPTER 11
TO THE SOUTH SEAS:
AUGUST-SEPTEMBER 1940

When I returned home to Hong Kong, Don left Chungking for Hong Kong soon after. He rented an apartment down the hill from the end of Kennedy Road towards the Happy Valley Racecourse. We were getting ready for our sailing adventure.

My diary:

Hong Kong, 21st August, 1940. We leave on 3rd Sept. and today came a despairing cry from Mr. D, "We have only 14 more days and I don't seem to be able to get started." He is referring to the packing. I sit among stacks of books and 'gear' and feel quite helpless. There is a typhoon on but Mr. D has gone to the sail makers, Wai Kee, to see if the ropes for the new sails for his yacht Mei Hwa [11] *are being immersed in linseed oil.*

I remember how hot and sticky it was and it was hopeless to open a window because the wind would wrench it from my hands.

---

[11] Mei Hwa means "Beautiful China."

Joyce and I went home from Don's flat and waited for the typhoon to pass.

I have lost my appetite. With the thousand and one things I have to remember and reading a badly printed pirated edition from Taiwan of Gone with the Wind *far into the night, my whole system feels sick.*

The movie of that story was playing at the King's Theatre and my friend Rose Kwok and I went to see it. She said a surprising thing, "Scarlet reminds me of you." I can see how prim and proper we all were (on the surface anyway), and I was different.

So far as the packing is concerned, I have filled four cases of tinned foods and one trunk. Mr. D gathered a lot of tools for Mei Hwa.

Don told me that he was planning to put the *Mei Hwa* aboard a steamer to the Solomon Islands, then sail her to Tahiti. That we were going to the South Pacific and not Indochina was a huge surprise. I had faith in Don that he knew what he was doing. It seemed so adventurous and romantic to sail off to the South Seas. I went out on the *Mei Hwa* only once as she was still not quite ready. There was a last minute change of rigging, from a yawl to a sloop.

Ah Cow (the young maid who came from our village to work for us, and who learned in no time to become a very good cook and a superb seamstress) *is now making three cheongsams for me, the thickest dresses I'll take. Also getting gray flannel slacks and a friend has knitted a thick grey sweater, just in case it gets cold in the South Seas. I only have my green trunk and the folding suitcase packed with plenty of shirts and shorts.*

I shall now write and tell Chieh about my leaving.

My mother, Chieh, was in Shanghai helping my sister Doris with her newborn son, Hon Ming. My heart ached that I would miss her by a few days. It turned out that I would not see her for over five years.

Sailing in Hong Kong Harbor 1940

Hong Kong, 2ⁿᵈ September, 1940. We sail tomorrow on the B & S [Butterfield & Swire] SS Yunnan. *The yacht* Mei Hwa *will be put on board. It's the first day of the 8th moon today and it's my Chinese birthday. I am 26 and beginning to feel a bit old. It's probably due to the packing.*

On board SS Yunnan, *4ᵗʰ September, 1940. We left yesterday at 6 p.m. The weather has been clear and the sea smooth. Rose and Ah Cow came on board on the 2:15 p.m. launch. We thought the Yunnan a neat and comfortable ship. In the main saloon was the card showing the list of passengers. When Rose saw this she laughed and laughed for all there was written on it was Mr. W. H. Donald and Miss A. Lee. And the Yunnan is a fair-sized ship!*

3 p.m. Mei Hwa *was maneuvered aboard. Don was there and looked happy when at last she nestled securely in her cradle. She seems so small without her mast. I took a dozen photos of her hanging in midair. Ah Fook* [Don's boat boy] *was there, clutching onto his umbrella.*

At dinner (8:30) I ate heartily and directly afterwards went to bed. My cabin is a roomy one, in fact, the best I've ever had on six sea trips of my life.

7ᵗʰ September, 1940. On the afternoon of the 5ᵗʰ, I felt seasick and stayed in bed till the morning of the 6th. My diet consisted of salted soda biscuits and practically nothing to drink. I think I have my sea legs now, anyway. It's quite calm with the long Palawan Island breaking up the beam sea.

Don and I started to study navigation and how to use the sextant to find our position at sea. It was fun learning the Morse code with all its *dits* and *dahs*. My cabin was next to the main saloon where everything took place and the officers and the two passengers had their meals. Since I was sea sick so much of the time, I left my door open and this kept me from isolation from the "outside" world. Don would study his navigation in the saloon while I drew a picture of him. We had a good Captain but after a while, we hardly saw him. I think he stayed in his cabin for days at a time.

14ᵗʰ September, 1940. I did not go ashore at Tarakan, [12] [Borneo, Indonesia] *our first port, on 9ᵗʰ September. Don said not to go. He was afraid I might have trouble coming back on board.*

---

[12] During World War II the island was captured (January 1942) by the Japanese and retaken by the Australians in May 1945. "Tarakan Island." Encyclopaedia Britannica Online. 28 Jan. 2009.
http://www.britannica.com/EBchecked/topic/583321/Tarakan-Island.

We shipped fuel oil to last the whole trip. The 3rd engineer tells me that she uses nearly 5 tons of oil a day.

After Tarakan the first bit of land we passed was Siau (Wed. September 11th) with a 6000 ft. volcano. On that day the ship

Ansie's sketch in her diary of Donald studying navigation
September 1940

started to roll again and I had to stay in bed the following day. The sunsets are lovely. This morning at about 5 a.m. we crossed the equator.

16th September, 1940. Madang, [13] New Guinea coast. We entered the harbour at sunset. This is such a pretty place. The

---

[13] Madang was abandoned by the British after 1914 because of the prevalence of malaria there. Australian administration after 1914 was followed in 1942-45 by Japanese occupation of the area. "Madang." Encyclopaedia Britannica Online. 28 Jan. 2009. http://www.britannica.com/EBchecked/topic/355664/Madang.

houses (bungalows) seem to be placed in a tropical garden with palm trees to shade every spot. The harbour is just like a lagoon with little islands dotted about.

Before leaving Hong Kong, I had researched some of our destinations, and had transcribed descriptions in my diary:

From the 1933 Handbook of the Western Pacific [Pacific Publications, Sydney]:

> MADANG is originally the centre of the German Administration. It is laid out in the form of a gorgeous tropical garden. There is a hotel and several stores in Madang, a small "Chinatown" and a swimming bath. Shore launch trips accommodate ten.

Visitors are not allowed to board. [A crew member had measles.] *The chief mate (Mr. Bennett) overcomes that by setting a dinner table right in the middle of the quay and instead of bringing the guests to dinner, dinner is brought to the guests.*

The natives are almost black and they look so colourful in their long cherry and vermilion lap laps. Tonight is full moon (15th day of the 8th moon), the moon rising like a yellow globe in a clear sky. Later it waxed lighter and brighter and the sea became quite lit up in rivulets of silver.

It is hot in the cabin, but there is not much to do after a short walk through the "town." There are about 30 foreigners and I think a dozen or so houses. Also there is the inevitable "Chinatown," which we visited in the moonlight.

The Chinese are from our district in south China and so we speak the same country dialect. When I told one of the shopkeepers my surname, he at once said "Lay Hay Sun," which is my Father's name. It made me feel suddenly homesick.

To this day, the mention of Madang brings up a sense of enormous peace after tribulation (those beam seas!) and memories of the full moon peeping through the palms and then transforming the lagoon into an iridescent jewel.

Salamaua, [14] *18th September. We arrived at Salamaua soon after lunch and left at 6 p.m. This port is placed in a long narrow strip of land with the sea on both sides. It is quite flat with bungalows and coconut palms along the one main road. We saw several lorries and a car. From here aeroplanes fly to Mau, the gold mines up the mountains. It is quite chilly out in the breeze.*

From the 1933 Handbook of the Western Pacific [ibid]:

> SALAMAUA, built since 1926, occupies the narrow isthmus which joins Parsee Cape to the mainland. Two miles away is the Salamaua Aerodrome where planes start for Goldfield's centres and for Lae on the other side of Huon Gulf—15 miles away.

Rabaul, [15] *20th-21st September, 1940. This port is full of cars and people who love the place. Mr. Spensley (the B & S agent) took Mr. D and me to his house for tea and later were driven to see the sights. The streets are lined with mango and casuarina trees. The shops ("Carpenters")* [an Australian retail chain] *look*

---

[14] Salamaua was captured by the Japanese in 1942 during World War II and later retaken by Australian and United States forces lead by General Douglas MacArthur on September 11, 1943 during the Salamaua – Lae campaign. During reoccupation the town was destroyed. Source: "Salamaua," *Wikipedia*. Retrieved 1/27/09.

[15] Occupied by the Japanese from 1942 to 1945, Rabaul was destroyed by Allied bombing; it was rebuilt after 1950. "Rabaul." Encyclopaedia Britannica Online. 28 Jan. 2009 http://www.britannica.com/EBchecked/topic/487869/Rabaul.

like homesteads, the same red and green colours of Madang. On the 21st [of September]*, Mr. D met the leading Chinese at the Kuomingtang hall and he gave them a talk about China. Later Mr. D went to have lunch with the Governor, Sir Ramsey Nicolls. Four women passengers are added to the list, one is Antonia Potts* [a friend from Hong Kong]. *She looks as fresh as ever and her twins are also on board.*

Directly leaving Rabaul (3 p.m.) the ship started to heave about. I suppose I will now have to change for dinner.

From the 1933 Handbook of the Western Pacific [ibid]:

> RABAUL, administrative centre of the Mandated Territory of New Guinea. Steamer berths at the western extremity of the town, a mile away from the chief business quarters. Cars can be hired. By following Malaguna Road parallel to the waterfront, one comes to the main stores and post office. By keeping straight on, one comes to Chinatown—two or three streets of Chinese shops. No other lines of shops and offices. 3 hotels. Tour of Rabaul: several, about 2 hour trips. Fare £1 to £2.

25th September, 1940. Arrived in the early hours at Nauru Island (just off the equator). Sea too rough to land coolies [Chinese workmen], *so stayed till 26th afternoon and went to Ocean Island (over 100 miles off).*

These two islands are covered with bird droppings, which had a world market as fertilizer.

30 September, 1940, on board SS Yunnan. *The yacht is clean at last. Mr. D has more or less sorted everything out. I have been busy copying charts of Tulagi and Gavutu harbour. Tomorrow we land. Antonia is sick with German measles. Mrs. Summerfield has malaria and the 3rd engineer looks like a ghost because of his cough. Rodney Potts has fever of 101; otherwise everyone is well.*

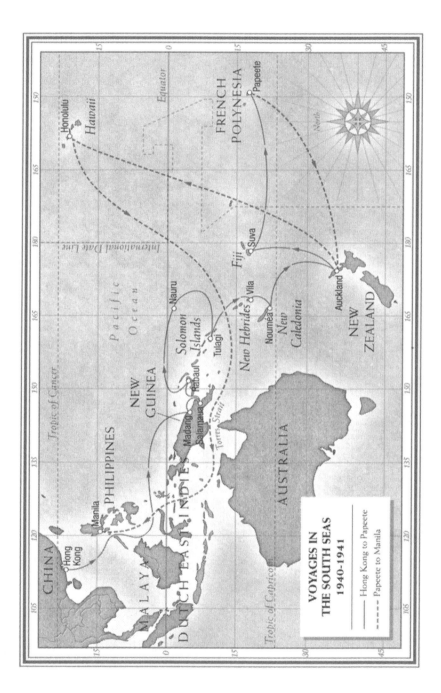

CHAPTER 12
TULAGI, SOLOMON ISLANDS:
OCTOBER-NOVEMBER 1940

From my diary:

1ˢᵗ October, 1940, Tulagi.[16] Arrived in sunshine before lunch. Lovely looking place.

From the 1933 Handbook of the Western Pacific [ibid]:

> TULAGI ISLAND, about three miles round, lying close to Florida Island. In harbour is small island of Makambo. Seat of government and port of entry for the Protectorate [of the British Solomon Islands].

We debarked SS *Yunnan* the next day. Don went to immigration to have our passports checked. The officer in charge told him they did not want any deadbeats. Don said he would take his yacht

---

[16] The town of Tulagi was the administrative seat (from 1893) of the British Solomon Islands Protectorate until it was destroyed by the Japanese (1942). The capital was subsequently moved to Honiara, a new town built on Guadalcanal. "Tulagi." Encyclopaedia Britannica Online. 25 Jan 2009
http://www.britannica.com/EBchecked/topic/608617/Tulagi.

elsewhere. Don did not tell me what ensued, but we were allowed to stay. Our treatment had repercussions in the British Foreign Office later.

I found out many years later that the British and Australian military intelligence were tracking Don's every move in the South Pacific, e.g. the letter reproduced below dated October 28, 1940, reporting on his arrival in Tulagi "accompanied by a Chinese lady secretary." This letter is one of many regarding Don that are in the Australian national archives.

DEPARTMENT OF DEFENCE

MINUTE PAPER.

(This side only to be written on.)

UBJECT: MR. W. H. DONALD.

CONFIDENTIAL.   28 OCT 1940

The Director of Military Operations
       and Intelligence.

The Director of Operations and Intelligence,
       AIR BOARD.

              Mr. W.H. Donald, who for some years past has been one of Chiang Kai Shek's principal advisors, arrived at Tulagi on 30th September, accompanied by a Chinese lady secretary.

2.   He has imported a yacht of approximately 14 tons, and states that he has come to the Solomon Islands to write his memoirs. It is not known how long he intends to remain in the Solomons, and he seems to have little to do with the local population, either European or Chinese.

Director of Naval Intelligence,
26th October, 1940.

29 OCT 1940

There was only one hotel and it was in Chinatown, and no girl would dream of staying there. Planters came from outlying islands to get drunk and raise hell. The resident doctor, Dr. Hetherington, and his kind wife came to the rescue and asked me to stay with them. I shall always be grateful to them. Don stayed on the *Mei Hwa*. Some Chinese had built a tiny cottage right on the water in their area, and Don rented it. Luckily, it was almost ready and I moved there before it was finished.

23ʳᵈ October, 1940. Tulagi. Have never been so hard-worked in my life. Cook all the meals and boil and wash clothes. Moved into a tiny house on a stone jetty in Chinatown and have just finished putting most of the things in their places.

"Boiling" clothes! Since I had never done any laundry in my life, except in a wash basin at Kweiyang while with the Medical Relief Corps, Don told me what to do. He said to boil water in a kerosene can, shave off some carbolic soap, and then boil the whole lot. Waiting for so much water to boil on a makeshift stove took a long, long time. Anyway, the clothes finished up looking gray and I was the same color with fatigue. They were so wrinkled they had to be ironed. Best not to go into that except to say that the iron I borrowed was heated by charcoal. Remember it was 1940 and although there was no drip dry clothing, I drip dried everything after the first few self-inflicted tortures.

Tonight the young lady (Liang) came early and said she couldn't stay. I feel really sad.

There was a small Chinese community in Tulagi, and we had asked one of the Chinese women to come help me around the house. But she probably disapproved of me because I was with Don.

When in a better mood I will write more about this pretty little island. Captain Wilson (70 and looks 50) came to supper tonight.

He introduced himself while we were returning from the hospital (Mr. D editing his films there). I get up now at 7 a.m. instead of 6 a.m. because this cottage is finished at last. The Chinese carpenters used to turn up at 6:30 a.m.

At the moment, Aliki, the boat boy turns up to wash up and sweep. The days are hectic and tiring. What an existence.

Tulagi, 27th October, 1940. Just for future reference, I brought away from Hong Kong A£33, HK$120 and US$200 in travelers' cheques.

Today, Sunday, has been my first "lazy" day. The Chinese children came after lunch and we tried to catch fish for my new kitten. One little fish was caught and eaten by the puss with relish. We saw a funny looking eel. It's hot today. This evening we go to dinner at Dr. Hetherington's and Mr. D is going to show his films.

Tulagi, 31st October, 1940. We landed here on the 2nd, so that makes our stay almost one month. I am so continually busy and then weary that I haven't the heart or strength to pick up a pencil to write my diary. Perhaps I should not say "heart," because I am having a terrifically interesting time. The wee house, Aliki the boat boy, and my attempts at cooking are one continual source of amusement.

I will tell you about the house first. It has a red roof, galvanized iron sheeting painted in red oxide. The rest of the house, outside and inside, and shutters are a bright eggshell blue. By a happy chance the two cane chairs and little table that Captain Summerfield (SS Yunnan) gave me match the front porch to perfection, as the reed shutters have edges of dark green and so have my chairs and table.

The cottage is built right on the water, and you approach it by walking from Chinatown along a man-made causeway of rocks and grass three feet wide. You reach the ramshackle shed of my neighbor first, then further out is my little house, looking spick and span in her new coat of paint. The house is joined to this path by a wooden bridge 25 feet long, and on Mondays you will see my washing blowing in the sea breeze on either side as you walk along the planks. I did not like the idea of hanging my undies and various garments right along the front bridge. As there was absolutely nowhere to dry my washing, the practical side of me won, and just in time for the Chinese carpenters to put up two wires before they finished their two-week job on the house.

There is a front porch, and five rooms: a bedroom, office, sitting/dining room, kitchen and bathroom. Also a little room at the back where Mr. D stores his things. He stays on his dream yacht, the Mei Hwa.

Today I did some furniture changing. The icebox and sideboard (both loaned by Mr. Hinchoy) were moved into the kitchen, and the wooden kerosene boxes for the kitchenware and tinned foods now sit snugly in the sitting room as the filing cabinet! When I have time I shall sketch the building. It is like a doll house.

The kitten came four days ago and now follows me around. The first two days I threw out my line and caught fish for her. Mr. D said she likes it raw, so I gave her three tiny fish. That evening she vomited from overeating and possibly indigestion. Now I cook her fish or meat and give her bread and milk for breakfast. Mr. Jack Ellis gave me the kitten.

Ever since we landed I have done all the cooking. [This is quite a statement since I had never before entered a kitchen.]

Then I have no servants except Mr. D's Aliki and as he states, "Me b'long sailor boy, me no b'long house boy." All the same he now comes faithfully every day after meals to wash up. He is a pet. Chocolate brown colour, well-built and has soft frizzy golden hair worn like a mop on top of his head. And a generous size mop it is too, with fresh flowers tucked in and coloured leaves dangling. The back of his head is closely shingled and unbleached. He is a cheery bloke and whistles while he washes up. He always whistles the same tune which is a jumble of many of the popular old songs like, "When the moon comes over the mountain." A number of the natives have ukuleles and harmonize and play English or American songs.

One afternoon while taking a stroll along the beach, we met a strapping native wearing a determined look on his face. He asked us gruffly, "Where you go Boss?" Don answered, "Just taking a walk," and politely asked him, "Where are you going?" "Me?" he replied, "Go Government House, play cricket."

You should see the natives play cricket on Saturday afternoons. In their bleached hair and coloured lap laps, it is an astonishing sight for a newcomer to watch them bowl and bat and behave like any sedate Englishman.

From Tulagi we took two overnight trips on the *Mei Hwa* and several shorter sails. Mr. Hinchong always came with us. He was a fairly young Chinese businessman living in Tulagi. Surprisingly, he said he had won a prize for dancing at one of the tea dances at the Hong Kong Hotel. What on earth was he doing in such a place as Tulagi?

Our first overnight trip was to Malaita Island, where we decided to go around the northern end. We met with headwinds and squalls and, after rounding the northerly coast, decided we had had enough, especially when Aliki and the two other boat boys managed to pull down the sails when the order was to shorten sail. We had an exciting time of it with all hands grabbing at the flapping canvasses, and the boom charging about in gale force winds.

We anchored off Savo Island.[17] Mr. Hinchoy slept soundly in the cabin, but I could not as it was so hot even at night, so the deck it was for me. I was told not to roll off the yacht in my sleep because there were plenty of sharks around. We also cruised along Guadalcanal and never saw any signs of life except wisps of smoke from a cooking fire.

The original plan had been to sail the *Mei Hwa* from the Solomon Islands to Tahiti. This ran into a snag when Don found out that, under old anti-blackbirding[18] laws, any crew he took on in the Solomons would not be allowed to leave the protectorate.

Reluctantly, he had to give up on that idea and shipped his beloved yacht back to Hong Kong. We made plans to continue by steamer to Vila, in the New Hebrides.

---

[17] Savo Island was bombed in early August, 1942, the first major naval engagement of the Guadalcanal campaign.

[18] Blackbirding: the 19th-and early 20th-century practice of enslaving (often by force and deception) South Pacific islanders on the cotton and sugar plantations of Queensland, Australia (as well as those of the Fiji and Samoan islands). Encyclopaedia Britannica Online. 25 Jan 2009 http://www.britannica.com/EBchecked/topic/68440/blackbirding.

Fishing off the *Mei Hwa*
Anchored off Savo Island, November 1940

CHAPTER 13
VILA, AUCKLAND & SUVA:
DECEMBER 1940-JANUARY 1941

From my diary written in Vila, one of the islands of the New Hebrides:

SS Morinda, *two thousand ton boat, thirty years old and should have been scrapped if it hadn't been for the war. We left Tulagi, Solomon Islands at 1 a.m. on the 5th* [of December, 1940] *and arrived at Vila (New Hebrides) in the morning of 9th December.*

We are trying to get to Auckland, New Zealand. This is the only route to go.

From the veranda of Madame Read's hotel one can see the whole of the Vila world go by. Desmoiselles flash pass in smart cars. Others in high heels and sleek kiss curls plastered on their foreheads walk with swinging gait along the sea front. Plump French children in brief skirts and shorts romp their way to school. Tonkinese maids, trim in their black and white uniforms, run errands for their mistresses. This morning, a vision of loveliness passed by on a chestnut filly. She wore a beautifully cut pair of dark green jodhpurs

Here in this British-French condominium, thousands of Tonkinese men work on plantations for two francs a day. Many of them hawk vegetables, piled in baskets swinging on long bamboo poles, balanced on toughened shoulders.

New Year's Eve, 1940. The Steamer Tegelburg *is due to arrive any minute now. We are off to Auckland. The stay here has been enjoyable but far too long.*

We were invited to a wedding by an Australian couple and looked forward to the feast as Madame Read's food had begun to pale. I said as much, and as usual should have kept my mouth shut; the banquet was catered by our dear Madame.

7th January, 1941. We have been waiting now for almost a month. At last there is news. The SS Tegelburg *arrives tomorrow morning. (War news: The raiders bombarded Nauru Island a week ago.)*

8th January, 1941. Left Vila at 1:30 p.m. and had 1st class "A" cabin with bathroom attached. I've an armchair and feel frightfully pampered!

Arrived at Nouméa on the 9th after lunch and stayed till 6 a.m. on the 11th. Had a lovely drive to the old 'fort' (there's nothing there!) I found Nouméa very lovely with its extensive seacoast. 11th and 12th, the sea being a little rough, I had to stay in bed. Oh, Mr. D danced with me for first time on the 10th evening. Poor dear developed his very first headache due to the sun, we think.

Good grief. Didn't China give him any headaches!

13th January, 1941. Due to arrive in New Zealand this evening. The Crumps have been our mealtime companions. Blandy and wife and twins are on board. the Resident Commissioner of Vila.

First day at Auckland lunched at Grand Hotel with Phil Delaney, Harold Gatty and W.H.D. Sitting behind me at next table was Noel Coward and a young man. I liked the Gattys and had my only decent meal at their house. There was rhubarb for dessert!

I enjoyed Auckland tremendously since the government welcomed W.H. Donald as an ambassador, though he had not planned it that way. (It was the very last thing on his mind, especially as he had walked away from all the work of advising China's head of state.) They gave him the royal treatment.

At Auckland we only had time for two cinemas: Blue Bird *and* Spring Parade*, and my first Gilbert and Sullivan opera*: Yeoman of the Guards.

Young Blandy took us and his parents to the Gilbert & Sullivan. I was enchanted, since I was familiar with the tunes. What a chuckle to see the antics on the stage!

Of course there was a Chinese meeting [with the overseas Chinese community in Auckland] *the night before we left (16ᵗʰ Jan) and W.H.D. must have been absolutely worn out with reporters. I had a perm at Milu & Choyce, which seemed frightfully expensive. Now I <u>really</u> feel a fool for not buying more clothes in Hong Kong. Chinese satin undies are worth their weight in gold. The little shop opposite our hotel (Waverley) said they were not allowed to import any more real silk.*

How did I know I would be thrown into high society? I thought I was going to sail around the South Seas in a yacht and all I needed was a change of underwear!

There was such a rush and a feeling of suspense to see if I could go to Tahiti. What an anticlimax to spend days, nay, months planning for a final destination only to learn that women were not allowed to travel on board the cargo ships heading for that distant place! But I must have been given special dispensation to travel, because on we went from Auckland to Suva en route to Tahiti.

Auckland to Suva

22nd January, 1941. On board cargo boat (USS Co.) [Union Steamship Company] *Waiotapu (over 3,000 tonnes and does 9-1/2 knots!)*

Well, here I am packing up to leave ship when she gets to Suva tomorrow. We left Auckland about midnight of the 17th Jan. and have had a very peaceful trip. There is one other passenger besides W.H.D. and myself. Stayed in bed for breakfast and lunch every day except today! (I am the world's worst sailor, except on a yacht when it is just inches above the water.) Have a very roomy double cabin to myself and the use of the captain's bathroom. He is very nice and has promised to buy some magazines from America for me to take to Tahiti on his next visit to the U.S. Chief steward bought flowers for my benefit. Second engineer mended my gramophone. Captain lent me magazines, as did wireless operator.

23rd January, 1941. Arrived Suva, Fiji Islands. Met Mr. Honson who took us for lunch at his house. Met Mr. Chen, Chinese consul and wife Kay, and David Donald, a relation of Don's from Australia with his young son.

24th January, 1941. Sir Harry Luke (Governor) asked me to go with W.H.D. to tea at 4:30 p.m. Went to Regal cinema with Mr. David Donald and W.H.D.

25th January, 1941. Meeting at Kuomintang to welcome W.H.D. at 3 p.m. Dinner at the Honsons' and some of W.H.D.'s films on the Japanese war on China were shown. Finished after midnight. Temperature 96 in the shade, and very humid.

Sunday, 26th January, 1941. Went for launch picnic with Chinese to a sand bank and there spent a hot hour looking at creatures on the reef. Dinner tonight with his Excellency, the

Governor. No clothes, except a black dress! This fits me well, thank goodness. Mrs. Honson sent flowers, so can wear a dark red rose with dress and gold bracelet.

At Government House, Sir Harry Luke was a very charming and genial host. He insisted I try the savory course, served after the sweet course, which was a big marrow bone on a piece of toast. I came up with my usual chatter and added, "Wasn't it a strange thing for the customs officer to say to a visitor on landing at Tulagi, 'We don't want any deadbeats here'?" For goodness' sake, how did I know that Sir Harry, in addition to being Governor of Fiji, was the High Commissioner for the Western Pacific and thus in charge of governing Tulagi as well? Apparently the usual customs man was away, and this fresh kid did the job. There was a dead silence and I can feel the chill to this day.[19]

Many years later, in the 1960s, my husband, Henry Sperry, was in charge of the First National City Bank of New York (now Citibank) in Hong Kong, and we were guests at Government House. The stately governor and I suddenly had a flash of revelation. "You are Ansie Lee?" I said, "You were in Tulagi?" That fresh kid in Tulagi turned out to have done alright after all. Oh well, all was not lost for the evening. Sitting beside me in the grand dining room was the guest of honor, a visiting Antarctic expedition leader, and he told me the secret of keeping my feet warm in freezing temperature. There is no need to wear heavy socks: the secret is to wear several layers of socks because it is the air between the layers that keeps you warm.

All trunks already on ship MV Limerick, *which is loading sugar at Lautoka, on the other side of the island, 160 miles away. Rains*

---

[19] Don had written about the rude reception we had received in Tulagi and the British Foreign Office in London had written to Sir Harry Luke asking him to follow up on it.

every day there; average annual rainfall 190 inches! Here, in Suva, people have Indians from India as servants.

SUVA TO PAPEETE

6th February, 1941. Sailed away from Fiji on Friday, 31st January, 1941. On board the ship to Tahiti, we are served tea at 5 p.m., which is the main meal of meat and potatoes, etc. Then supper at 8:30 p.m., when we get sandwiches and tea. Crossed the International Dateline next day so it was Friday 31st again! This boat, MV Limerick, *is as steady as a rock. So far I have not been sick once. I think we are due in Papeete tomorrow morning. It has taken us two months and two days to travel from Tulagi in the Solomon Islands to Papeete, Tahiti. Perhaps on Don's yacht it would have been a bit quicker, but what a lot of interesting people we would have missed.*

CHAPTER 14
FRENCH POLYNESIA: FEBRUARY-JULY 1941

On Friday, February 7, 1941, the MV *Limerick* arrived at the island of Tahiti, and docked at the waterfront of its capital, Papeete. Tahiti - at last! I followed Don down the gangplank. Greeting us on the wharf was a Chinese man, his skin smooth and light. He was of medium height, and he spoke English without an accent.

"Welcome, Mr. Donald, and welcome, Miss Lee." He introduced himself as Siu. (I could not hear his full name, but later found he was known as Ah-You or Monsieur Ah-You.)

Don and I were astonished by the welcome we received. There was a big gathering of Chinese at the quay, with a large banner that spelled out "Welcome Mr. W.H. Donald and Miss Ansie Lee." There was music, and school children singing songs of welcome. What a surprise! As Monsieur Ah-You told us later, the Chinese community was really excited about W. H. Donald's visit. They were so far away from their homeland, yet the Advisor to Generalissimo Chiang Kai-Shek was visiting them, giving them plenty of "face" to the local French government's officials.

A welcome from the Chinese community in Papeete, February 7, 1941
W.H. Donald & Ansie are in front row, holding flowers

Now the Chinese felt they were not neglected by their country, and they hoped that in the future they would be treated with greater courtesy and respect.

Along the quay, in front of the warehouses and shacks, there were long benches, and here the children waited for us to step down from the gangplank. The children from the Chinese school began to sing, and a string of firecrackers sparked the air accompanied by a burst of sound. It was thrilling and made me think of Chinese New Year. There were many more speeches that day at a dinner party that was held in the hall of the Chinese School. The whole room was filled with long tables for the French guests, as well as the Chinese community.

The main citizen of the Chinese community was Monsieur Ah-You. He was born near Canton in the village of Loong Kong and went to Hong Kong's Queen's College for schooling, where my father had been a student. Later, he and his bride came to settle in Papeete, Tahiti. He was medium height with a youthful, cheerful, round face. He and Mrs. Siu (Siu was his surname) had several children who were later sent abroad to America for college and became some of the most influential citizens of Tahiti. Monsieur Ah-You had a large general goods store and his wife could sew men's clothes, as well as ladies'. I remember seeing a big rowboat in the loft of the shop "in case of floods and storms, so my family would not be drowned." Monsieur Ah-You took care of us in every way and rented for us a beautiful house in the district of Paea, 13 ½ kilometers from Papeete. The house was referred to as "Chez Menzies."

Across the sea from our house was the island of Moorea, whose mountains formed the silhouette of a reclining maiden. As evening fell, her perpetual pose of abandonment was bathed in a warm glow as the sun sank into the ocean.

It was at Paea, in days long past, that Polynesian kings took delight in surfing the huge rollers as the waters raced to the shore, leaving a spread of white lace on the lava sands. They brought this pastime with them to the Hawaiian Islands.

Mr. Menzies, a Canadian, had built this thatched-roof house near the beach separated from the main road by a large coconut plantation. We let light and air into the house by pushing out sturdy matting, the size of large windows and about three feet from the floor, using poles to anchor the mats. The dwelling stood on stilts, close to a pebbly beach, surrounded by a raised flower bed of white impatiens with red centers.

To our surprise, there was hot water all day in the bathroom for showers, but no sign of a hot water heater anywhere. Solar heating was the magical source of power. Coils of piping were laid on top of a small trellis outside the house. The tilt of the coils lets the water, heated by the sun and warm air, slowly trickle into an insulated storage tank.

Inside Chez Menzies, there were two bedrooms and a large sitting room, with a few steps leading down to the dining room. Along these steps was a built-in bookcase, and among the books was a Cordon Bleu cookbook in English. Here, at this unlikely time and place, my life-long joy of cooking began.

The kitchen was modern, with a large gas-burning refrigerator and appliances that were up-to-date for the year 1941. My Tahitian cat would sit on the ledge of the window (the only glass window), turning his head now and then to stare at my attempts to prepare a new dish. Tu, our willowy maid, kept the kitchen clean. "Madame," a chieftain's daughter, did the rest of the house cleaning and the laundry.

The dining table was just outside the kitchen, and I have pleasant memories of simple suppers of cottage pie, custards and other English dishes that Don liked. I was familiar with them from my school days in England. Don's reputation in China was that he never ate any Chinese food. He never drank any kind of liquor. When others toasted with champagne, his glass looked like champagne, but I knew it was ginger ale. His favorite drink was a cup of strong tea with plenty of sugar.

Chez Menzies, Paea, Tahiti 1941

From my diary:

Moved to Chez Menzies on 12th Feb. and have now almost settled down. Coping with the servant question, having just employed Mary in place of Tu as cook. Madame came to us as a housekeeper and is the daughter of the Chief of the next district, Papara. She has a broad face, rather dark, and looks like one of Gauguin's paintings. She is tall and stands very straight and has a warm smile. We liked each other right away. With her is a young-looking husband, small-boned, pale and thin, and a young son, also rather frail. The ménage live in a tiny cottage that is part of the estate. Madame cleans the house and does the laundry. None of the natives here speak English, which is fine with me as our second language at the Diocesan Girls' School in Hong Kong was not Chinese, but French.

Don dictates lots of letters for the mail, which is supposed to go when the cargo boat from New Zealand comes in, but only once a month.

27th March, 1941. Two days ago, two big cruisers and four destroyers steamed along the horizon. What a thrill for everyone. They are American and will leave this morning. On the 22nd of last week, the Cheng Ho *left Papeete with Mrs. Anne Archbold.*

Don and I were invited to lunch on the *Cheng Ho* and I was enthralled with Mrs. Archbold's sense of adventure to be sailing these vast seas in a junk. The junk was built in Hong Kong and was constructed of beautiful teak wood.

Cheng Ho was indeed an apt name for this seafaring craft. Cheng Ho was a 14th century eunuch in the court of the Ming emperor. He was so bright that at the age of thirty he was commissioned to be the Commander-in-Chief of the Western Oceans. His first journey was in 1405 with sixty-two ships and 27,000 men. On later adventures, he sailed to southwest India and as far west as the Gulf of Arabia. He collected spices and exotic animals, and brought back to China envoys from more than thirty states of south and southeast Asia to pay tribute to the Emperor. He made seven voyages almost one hundred years before Vasco de Gama began his voyages of discovery. After Cheng Ho's death in 1435, a new Ming emperor terminated expeditions abroad. His "Middle Kingdom" had no need for the outside world.

8th April, 1941, Paea, Tahiti. Last night was chilly for the first time, and this morning I had breakfast early at 7:30 a.m. and felt the thrill of the change of weather. Just like a Hong Kong autumn day.

Easter Day, 13th April, 1941, Paea, Tahiti. The cold didn't last and I have taken off my blanket. Am now fixing up photos of our journey. Just received letters from family, Joyce and Dick. It's hot.

Don taught me how to ride a bike. (In Hong Kong no one rode bicycles; it's too hilly.) There were many laughs and spills as I practiced on our spacious grounds, trying not to get conked on the head by a falling coconut. Soon, we rode our bikes every day and my first trip was to go into town to visit the Coster family. I was so nervous as it was over thirteen kilometers. After that I was not afraid anymore. Going south we dropped in at Mr. Giles's big estate to listen to the many songs and cries of the birds he had brought over from different parts of the world. He fed them, but they were all free to come and go as they pleased.

Each kilometer was marked by a stone on the side of the road starting from Papeete going south. There was little traffic. But as the sun rose, "Le Truck" always headed for town, rattling its wood benches, the gears screeching as it braved an incline near our house. Mid-morning, a horse-drawn cart driven by a Chinese man passed our house, and the man would stuff fragrant baguettes into metal boxes outside each home. He came again in the afternoon.

School children always greeted us with a cheery, high-pitched, "Bon jour, M'sieur, Dame" and waved enthusiastically. A couple of times when tourists were visiting (off cargo ships), I would wear a pareu, often a blue one with large white breadfruit leaves printed all over it, and pose by our house. (What's so romantic about a Chinese girl in front of our estate? So I went native. Fortunately, the distance from the entrance was too great to distinguish my face.) The ships from New Zealand came only once a month and one time Mr. Hall (of Nordiff and Hall) came with a thoughtful gift: toilet paper, as the shops had run out and the ship was not due for some time.

TRIP TO TUAMOTUS AND MARQUESAS

17th April, 1941, at home in Paea. Well, here I am all of a dither packing again. This time a trip on a schooner to the Marquesas! We start tomorrow, that is if Mr. D (who is in town) can get the permission of the Governor in time. The cost for the trip is 100 francs a day for each of us for about three weeks.

On Saturday, April 19, 1941, the schooner *Vaitere*, a motor sailor, left Papeete at 9:15 a.m. for the Tuamotus. Don and I were on board.

The Tuamotu Archipelago lies east of Tahiti and stretches in a north-westerly direction. The atolls and coral reefs with seventy-eight islands are all lined with coconut palms since the dried meat of the latter, copra, is their one and only money crop. In later years, they farmed oysters for their black pearls. Except for the raised coral island of Makatea, with its phosphate deposits, the rest of the land is only three to five feet above the sea. There are lagoons, large and small, ringed by necklaces of islets with fine white sandy beaches. The trapped waters are teeming with fish, including sharks and manta rays. Here it truly looks like "The South Seas."

Monday, 21ˢᵗ April, 1941. Takaroa, Tuamotus. Dropped anchor at our first port at 6 a.m. After drinking my first cup of weak coffee, went for a stroll around the village. Very spick and span. The women dressed as in Papeete, colourful pareus plus skimpy tops. (Only one wrinkled old woman did not cover her bosom.) The simple dwellings are made of wood and most needing paint. All houses have tin roofs to catch rain water. Here the natives are short of food, so they eat coconuts, fish, dogs and pigs. We brought them some flour and sugar. Everyone looks well-fed, however, and happy. One passenger got off.

The Captain warned us that we will meet one of his wives. He has three or four. One came to see him off at Papeete.

He was one of the most handsome Tahitians we met, and had a "wife" in every port!

The *Vaitere* left the Tuamotus and headed north-east towards the Marquesas Archipelago. We plowed through fairly strong seas for two full days and three nights. I was seasick and did not eat the entire time.

The Marquesas islands of French Polynesia lie 1,250 kilometers northeast of Tahiti. There are ten islands of volcanic origin, and some coastlines have land jutting straight up from the sea piercing the clouds with their jagged peaks. With no coral reef or coastal plains, the natives live along narrow and deep valleys fed by mountain streams. There are few calm anchorages.

This archipelago lies within the doldrums of the equator and few sailing crafts made their way here. The natives came from Polynesian mariners from Tonga some 2,000 years ago. In 1595, Alvarado Mendana, ,a Spanish explorer, came upon the southerly islands and named them "Marquesas" for the Marquesa de Mendoza.

In 1774, Captain Cook arrived at Fatu Huku in the center of the chain. Whalers and slave ships arrived later and with them, the dreaded diseases of the "civilized" world, cutting down the population of 50,000 to 1,200 in fifty years. France annexed the Marquesas in 1842.

24th April, 1941. Omoa, Fatu Hiva, the southern tip of this archipelago. We arrived here early this morning. This valley is fertile and has everything in the way of fresh food. Juicy sweet oranges are now in season. There are mango trees, citron, papaya, bread fruit, bananas (also red ones for baking, we had them for lunch), cows, chickens, horses, pigs, turkeys, geese, and goats. At the moment we can see wild goats scampering on the mountain crags. The valley is damp and the grassland lush; coconut palms afford wide expanses of shade.

Lounging comfortable on the Vaitere *afterdeck, Don and I watched the steward through binoculars. He is in the water, wearing tight little goggles and has a spear with a line attached. I also hold my breath as he slips under the water, but give up long before his head comes up gasping for air. At the end of his spear is a wriggling shiny red fish. From a distance, four of the ship's crew are peering into the water on a ledge of the precipice holding spears. They have already impaled a couple of fish. We will have* poissons frites *for lunch.*

Sup-Cargo, M. Courlon, exchanges his empty gasoline tins for chickens and fruit. Chickens are valued on this trip at 12 francs each, but it's different each time. He buys them to feed us and his crew. We have a good cook and everything is fresh. This trip is a delight and we are part of the family.

Friday, 25ᵗʰ April, 1941, Atuona, Hiva Oa. This morning arrived here before daybreak and had to bounce about in mid-ocean for half an hour before embarking for this valley. There are Chinese here and one of them took us to the ancient sacrificial place. (Females are taboo.) He showed us the exact spot where humans were sacrificed. This spot is neglected (no tourists!) and overgrown with weeds.

Saturday, 26ᵗʰ April, 1941, Paumau Bay, Hiva Oa. Staying here till tomorrow. It is cool, not cold like the first night, and we plan to sleep under the stars on top of the salon. The sea air is a tonic against motion sickness as the anchorages are not always calm, and being cooped up behind a drawn curtain in the bunk in the salon is awful for me. But this is the rainy season, so we have to be ready to rush below with our bedding at the first drop of rain. If Captain needs to weigh anchor in the night, he can steer and peer past my head, just a couple of feet away.

The salon where we had our meals was also where we slept. There were bunks around the room and curtains for privacy. There was one tiny toilet and no means of washing. On most days we anchored in some quiet bay, and I would walk up the valley to a stream and just dive in.

This morning we met Mr. Lee, a Norwegian working for Donald's, a general store (no connection with W.H.D.) He ran away from a sailing ship 33 years ago. Speaks English and was most kind, his wife giving me a bunch of yellow roses and red cannas, a watermelon and lots of young coconuts. Their eldest son took us to see the biggest tikis in the Marquesas in their original surroundings. In this shaded spot were six tikis, three of which were in prone positions.

Sunday, 27ᵗʰ April, 1941, Nuku Hiva. The Bishop and princess, fellow passengers, got off at this valley. Taiohae is the seat of administration for the Marquesas and the only settlement we have seen. Today being Sunday, crew and all did just as they pleased. We went for a walk. Here there is a prison, a hospital (the administrator being its doctor) and telegraph office. There is the usual lone Chinese here with his store. He came on board and gave me a carved rosewood bowl and a sandalwood walking stick for Mr. D. No copra here, so next day, Monday morning, the boat loaded tree trunks nearby. This wood is the tong. It is the best wood here for furniture. The loading took till about 4 p.m., so steamed to Typee Valley for the night.

At 1 a.m. started for Ua Pou, 27 miles off. Now Tuesday, 29ᵗʰ April. This island rises up from the sea with jagged cliffs and has the highest mountain of the Marquesas with several narrow valleys running to the sea. Children play in the sea, many coming out to the boat in midget dugouts (some had outriggers). Saw the junk Humel Humel *with a person and a Chinese girl on board.*

Wednesday, 30ᵗʰ April, 1941. We are back at Nuku Hiva loading copra. This morning early we had a few native women on board. For lunch the crew caught about thirty fish, including a baby shark. Also shot a wild cow. Anchored again at Typee.

3rd May, 1941, Typee, Nuka Hiva. All the early hours were spent by crew trying to get the rudder out of the mud. Succeeded at daybreak (5:30 a.m.). I was filled with excitement to think I would be walking into this romantic place that Herman Melville had described in his book, Typee. *Went ashore at 7 a.m. and walked with Mr. D, Mlle. Rose and her bonne [maid] up this long and fertile valley. They dropped back after one hour but we continued for another half-hour when we saw a very high waterfall across the other side of the vast valley. Here the land is planted with coconut, breadfruit, banana, taro, papaya, pumpkin, orange and lime. I feel as if I have been here before. What an odd thought. Saw only two women and a few children on the walk.*

The Vaitere *motored to the next valley and as there was no cargo for shipment, soon came back to this chief bay, Taiohae, where everyone but Don and I rushed ashore in the light of the waxing moon.*

8th May, 1941, Atuona, Hiva Oa 7:30 p.m. We have just come aboard after staying two days and a night on shore. We were with Mr. Bob MacKiltrick. After lunch we three visited Paul Gauguin's grave and found that he died this very same day in 1903. Was it a propitious omen? I said a little prayer for the man who left the world such rich paintings. Later two small truckloads of natives came to see us off and, my word, I had to leap from the pier to a whale boat to take us back to the Vaitere, *heaving offshore. Moon three-quarters full.*

For sixteen days we chugged from one bay to another, mainly hauling huge logs, and collecting whatever goods we could. On board were forty pigs, thirty goats, eleven head of cattle, some sheep and chickens. There was copra too, with its sickly sweet rancid smell seeping through the hold. Since our boat was less than a hundred feet long, every bit of deck space produced squeals, bleatings and odd noises. Only the cows remained calm. Often there was no business at all, and then the crew would gleefully take to the cliffs with their one rifle. Mostly they scrambled after goats and they bragged that nary a shot was ever wasted. On hearing a "bang" we knew that it would be stewed "lamb" for dinner.

9th May, 1941. Fatu Hiva, our first and last island in the Marquesas. We are going back home.

We left Virgin Bay and Omoa Bay for Takaroa in the Tuamotu Archipelago. We took on a final load: a thin lad with watery eyes and the Chief of Omoa with his handsome young wife and baby daughter. Now there are six passengers with two round-trippers, Don and me.

We headed for Tahiti the way we came, via the Tuamotu Archipelago. There were head winds and a strong sea, and we barely made six knots with our powerful engine. After two days of tossing, we thankfully made port at Takaroa.

12ᵗʰ May, 1941. Takaroa again. M. Courlon sold a few smelly billy goats to another schooner here, and he says that covers the expense of the whole herd. On the oranges he has made a profit of a thousand francs already. He traded the last of his empty gasoline cans for chickens. They are scrawny birds, and though chicken is our daily diet, the Tahitian cook makes it delectable with taro or green papaya or baked with breadfruit, but always smothered in garlic.

We are only staying here till after mid-day. I went ashore and walked along the sandy stretch to take a fresh-water shower at Mr. Palmer's house. I had met him when we touched Takaroa on our outward bound trip. A Chinese store keeper gave me some pearls, one large one, also some pearl shells. It is so hot here, with plenty of flies. Quite suddenly, the wind started to whistle past my ears and the palms of the coconut tried frantically to rip away from their trunks. Captain sent a boy to round us up and said we must leave as soon as possible. He and the crew did not eat lunch but battened down the hatches and tried to make everything fast. M. Courlon joined us at the dining table.

"The worst place," he said, "in the whole South Seas is to be among the Tuamotus in a hurricane. These islands are only a couple of feet above sea level and there are many of them. You would not even see them from a short distance if there were no palm trees."

We soon pulled up anchor, and the *Vaitere* rolled and pitched so badly I immediately took to my bunk. The Chief of Omoa and his wife, not having their sea legs, became violently ill. Soon the salon became fetid as all portholes were closed. Two of the dining chairs became untied from the lines and crashed about.

It did not take long before I felt I could not breathe, so I forced myself out of the bunk and scrambled up the few steps to the door. I had to give it a mighty push before it opened a few inches. Out at last, the door slammed shut and I was struck by the scene and the voice of the Captain, yelling at me, *"Attention, tenez fermement!"* He was only a few feet away, dripping wet from head to toe and standing frozen to the wheel.

The next moment there was a lurch, and the whole sea swept across the deck almost knocking me off my feet. We're sinking, I thought, not really caring. How cool the seawater feels. I was gripping the handrail near the cabin door as the *Vaitere* shook herself clear of the sea. Then she climbed toward the inky nothingness, paused a moment, and slid down to the next trough.

Suddenly, an anguished voice from the bow shouted something in Tahitian, and our Captain spun the large spokes of the steering wheel around. For a moment we had almost run aground. With the change of direction, the boat wallowed in the valley, and a mountainous wave swept in relentlessly to swallow us up. All I could see was a line of white spume atop a black moving mass. I shut my eyes, squeezing out the salt water, or was it tears? Next thing I heard was a chuckle from our Captain, and when I looked again, we were riding on top of that fearsome wave. The boat was once again headed on a safer course.

For an age, I clung to the railings until at last we swept perilously close to the last of the islands. After that, the sea was rough, but predictable, and all hands were taken off the look-out posts. Our salon was sluiced down, and I was ordered back to the salon. One more night of angry seas before we crept through the entrance in the harbor at Papeete on May 14, 1941.

THE "RAIATEA TOUR"

While in town for the July 14th Bastille Day celebrations, Don received a telegram from Madame Chiang telling him to come back to China. He asked Monsieur Ah-You to make plans for chartering a schooner to take us to Honolulu. But first, at Monsieur Ah-You's request, we went on a tour to visit the Chinese communities on several of the Leeward Society Islands: Huahine, Raiatea and Bora Bora.

The next few days were busy. From my diary:

13th July, 1941. Went into town to stay a night at the Stuart Hotel. The whole town is already celebrating Bastille Day. Saw booths (similar to other fairs) and went to dinner at the Costers' home. There was a public ball outdoors and native dancers from our district of Paea who won first prize. It made us feel so proud. The town of Papeete is alive with music and laughter everywhere!

14th July, 1941. Monsieur Ah-You wants Don to visit the Chinese communities in the other Society Islands. At 7:30 p.m. we boarded the 115-ft Benecia *for our tour. What a strange looking vessel with many decks; it served as a ferry for the Society Islands. Its ungainly shape and height caused it to pitch and wallow in any but the calmest seas.*

15th July, 1941. Arrived at Huahine at 9 a.m. and stayed one hour. Another four hours to the island of Raiatea. It has been arranged that we stay one week in a new little house by the sea. The Chinese community was so kind and wanted to make us happy. The

*community here is from our district in south China and I feel quite
proud to be one of them.*

*16ᵗʰ July, 1941, Raiatea. It is 6 p.m., and already too dim to
read. There is no electricity in the house. Dinner is being brought
in. I hope it is not such a mess as lunch or breakfast. Wobbly fried
eggs, beefsteak and a dozen hard-boiled eggs! The daughter of the
owner of this house, Mlle Hart, manages the household. She is
plump and obliging. Thank goodness I speak French. This morning
borrowed bicycles and we rode along the seashore. It's hot in the
sun but there is a strong breeze. The* Benecia *will return in a week.*

*19ᵗʰ July, 1941, Raiatea. Yesterday, Friday at noon was the
official reception for Mr. D. I was feeling pretty sick, mainly from
our diet. Don's talk, with Monsieur Ah-You translating into his
native Chinese dialect, lasted one hour. There was much
enthusiastic applause. We were on an outdoor platform with the
"Welcome to Mr. W.H. Donald and Miss Ansie Lee" hanging
overhead. (I suppose they carried it from Papeete with the
entourage.)*

*23ʳᵈ July, 1941, Bora Bora. After four hours very rough weather
we arrived at Bora Bora at 4:30 p.m. and are staying at a house
belonging to a Chinese storekeeper.*

*24ᵗʰ July, 1941. Went for drive. This island is small with huge
rocks piled in the middle. At 4 p.m. there was a party in honour of
Don. There was Tahitian dancing to the rhythm of a kerosene can
and a block of wood. Three women and eight men performed,
shimmying and shaking every part of their bodies. To watch them
made one tingle all over. Whoever thought of such dancing!*

*Everyone wore wreaths of flowers. There were 50 for dinner,
some French, about twenty Chinese and our entourage of ten. Don
made an outstanding speech and Monsieur Ah-You translated it into*

Tahitian. We sat under a leafy hall built for the occasion. The sun sparkled on the sapphire lagoon as its waters lapped nearby.

At the moment Don is listening to the London news. This afternoon we heard America's threat to Japan about occupying Indochina. Our schooner Benicia *leaves at midnight.*

26th July, 1941. Yesterday we were at Huahine, our last island. Today we arrived back to Tahiti at 5 p.m. from the "Raiatea Tour." It was blowing hard all the way with headwinds. The journey took twenty-three hours instead of twelve. I lay in my bunk all the time. Don said he did too, as he could not get out due to all the seasick people lying about the saloon.

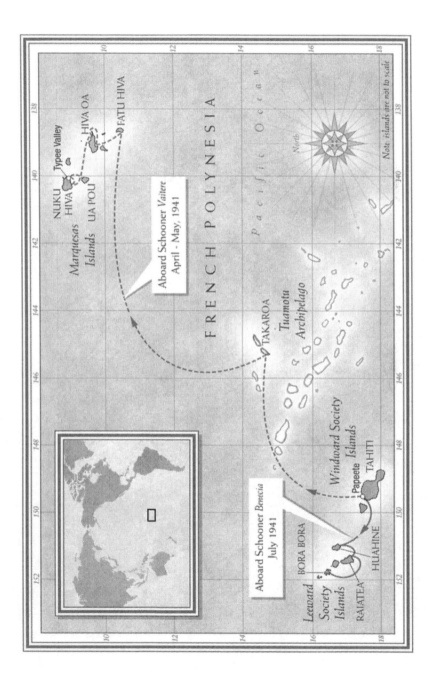

FRENCH POLYNESIA

Pacific Ocean

Note: islands are not to scale

North

Marquesas
Islands

NUKU
HIVA

UA POU

Typee Valley

HIVA OA

FATU HIVA

Aboard Schooner *Vaitere*
April - May, 1941

TAKAROA

Tuamotu
Archipelago

Windward Society
Islands

Papeete

TAHITI

Aboard Schooner *Benicia*
July 1941

Leeward
Society
Islands

BORA BORA

RAIATEA

HUAHINE

CHAPTER 15
TAHITI TO HONOLULU:
AUGUST–OCTOBER 1941

From my diary:

28th July, 1941, Paea, Tahiti. It's sunny, dry and cool. I am wearing a jersey and thick linen pants. How windy it is these days. Last night the whole house had to be shut up otherwise there would have been draughts. Don had slight temperature but is all right this morning. We had a hearty breakfast at 8:30 a.m. (later than usual; 7:30 a.m. is the time when there's work to do). Ate two fried eggs and bacon, two cups coffee with fresh milk.

Don has just come out to sit in sun. He is reading Life *and has two jerseys on.*

15th August, 1941, Paea, Tahiti. Just rode back from town. Don has finally decided that we will not take the schooner trip to Honolulu with Mr. Crane. This Florence Robinson *leaves on the 19th. He thinks I won't be able to stand the long trip on a ninety-foot schooner if I had to come back to Tahiti on her due to outbreak of war. I am rather sorry we are not going, but it's all for the best.*

Well, here we are all packed, and we hope to be able to get passage on the next Union Steamship. But, confidentially, this ship has been requisitioned by the government to take off crooks to New Zealand. However, I hope we can manage to get on board.

We did manage to get passage on the next Union Steamship Company ship, which turned out to be the S.S.*Waiotapu*, back to Auckland. From there we took another ship to Honolulu.

The news re coming conflict between Japan and America and England is still very uncertain, and yesterday we heard what declaration Roosevelt and Churchill had to make after their dramatic meeting in mid-ocean.

12th September, 1941, Paea, Tahiti. "Our" steamer due in 15th Sept. We are all packed except for odds and ends. However today, after much thought and deliberation, Don rings up Eddie and Mr. Coster to say we are not going if no telegram comes from Chungking (in answer to Don's 2,000 franc telegram, twenty-five words in code.)

14th September, 1941, Paea Tahiti. Sunday. What a lovely day! The first fresh day in weeks. After the heavy rainfall the air is crystal clear and clean. The sun is bright. Today is our last Sunday here. The Waiotapu *arrives tomorrow.*

15th September, 1941, Paea, Tahiti. We leave Tahiti today— maybe, if the ship is in. It's a lovely morning, the reef quiet.

9 a.m. All sorts of people are sitting about the house. Mrs. Kong came with truck for luggage but we had already sent twenty pieces to town to Ah-You's. The Beckers came and took away some gifts. Louise is sitting about with Tu and Madame. She brought me a hat.

16th September, 1941, Papeete, Tahiti. Spent last night at Mr. & Mrs. (Auntie Win) Costers and with Daisy, their daughter. Wore new Bata shoes; they hurt my toes. Bicycled about the town. Went to bank to declare money taken out and found we needn't (so long as one is not taking out more than one brought in). Had lunch upstairs at Ah-

You's shop and at 2:30 p.m. took our twenty-eight pieces of luggage to the customs. The chief didn't turn up till 3:30 p.m., and then we turned in our declaration of money that we first signed on landing. Don gave a slip showing how much he took out. They did not bother about the bags only things we brought out of the island again. Fortunately I remembered the exact number of records I sold to Mrs. Kong because these were taxed earlier. This afternoon they deducted those I had sold from the whole and asked me to produce ten records. I had given one to Eddie (Ernest Edmond) but anyway there were just ten in my trunk.

Yesterday from 3:30 p.m. to 5:30 p.m. Don and I made the rounds of the three schools. Had dinner with the captain of our steamer at the Costers. We are deluged with mission mangoes. People began to know that Don likes mangoes and now we have over two small boxfuls. Marie Lee [Ah-You's married daughter] made me a silk blouse and presented me with a pretty piece of coral.

Due to the crew not turning up in time, we have to leave early on the 17ᵗʰ September.

We are on the SS Waiotapu *again. In the best cabin as before and making a couple here furious for not getting it. He says he'll get Coster the sack for this!!*

Meals on board are:

> *6:30 am. morning tea in cabin (I don't take)*
> *8 a.m. breakfast*
> *10:30 a.m. tea**
> *12 noon dinner (not called lunch)*
> *3:30 p.m. afternoon tea (biscuits)**
> *5 p.m. tea (not called supper though it's like a heavy dinner, only without soup or dessert*
> *8:30 p.m. supper (tea, sandwiches and biscuits)*
>> ** not usually taken by me*

These times are the same on all the Union S. Ships; something about the convenience of the stewards.

21ˢᵗ September, 1941. On board SS Waiotapu. *Yesterday was my birthday so opened the Heidsieck magnum of champagne for 8:30 p.m. supper. It tasted wonderful. Today I ate heartily for first time and didn't even feel a little sick. Poor Don has a toothache but the pain stopped after taking an Empirin.*

Weather calm, sunny and following winds. Cargo 6 (?) bombers camouflaged. This ship is very steady, burns coal and throbs like a heartbeat.

The SS *Waiotapu* was carrying military aircraft bombers on board.

At sea, Sat. 27ᵗʰ, September, 1941. Crossing the dateline we skipped a Friday (yesterday). That makes me about equal since going east we had two Fridays!

This trip has been enjoyable. (But Mr. D. has toothache.) The weather is really cold and I am wearing my new grey flannel trousers and thick grey sweater. We are in sight of the mainland [New Zealand] *this evening and the Captain asked us up on the bridge to watch the paravanes[20] being lowered.*

1st October, 1941. Arrived Auckland Sunday. We were met by Mr. Furlong, representative of the government and government car is at Mr. D's disposal. Went up to the Museum. The Maori section is most interesting.

This evening we are going down by the 7:15 p.m. night train to Wellington (on the government). Trip takes till about 9 am tomorrow. It is cold enough for a fur coat but I won't buy a coat and wait till Shanghai or Hong Kong.

---

[20] Paravane: a torpedo-shaped protective device with serrate teeth in its forward end used underwater by a ship in mined areas to sever the moorings of mine. In *Merriam-Webster Online Dictionary*. Retrieved January 23, 2009, http://www.merriamwebster.com/dictionary/paravane

The government treated Don like a VIP, and I was accorded the same courtesies. Can you imagine my surprise when I was escorted to pay visits to several organizations of which they were most proud, designed to help their citizens improve their health and living standards? One of them was a dental school. The Minister of the Interior himself drove us to visit their famous sights, hot springs, etc.

We toured Rotorua and its geysers, Waitomo, where I was impressed by the glow worm caves, then Wairakei and Lake Taupo.

Best of all was going to the home of Mr. Peter Fraser, the Prime Minister, to attend a party for their Maori soldiers who had just returned from fighting for the Allies in Europe. I went alone and was greeted at the door by the Prime Minister's wife herself. When we proceeded to the kitchen, I asked her, "Don't you have anyone to help you?" She replied, "Have you not noticed how much older the wives look in this country?" She meant, I suppose, that there is no servant class. Then we proceeded to go out into the garden where the returned veterans were gathered for dinner.

When I was in Berkeley, California after the war in 1945, I was honored to receive a telephone call from Mr. Peter Fraser. He said that I would be most welcome to come live in New Zealand, and he offered me citizenship. This was at a time when New Zealand's immigration laws still discriminated against the Chinese.

From my diary:

19th October, 1941. Auckland. Tomorrow 20th, we sail on the Mariposa *(Matson Lines) for Honolulu. The* Mariposa *has been requisitioned by the government to carry airmen to America for further training. There will be nearly 2,000 on board (including crew). We got passage through Mr. P. Fraser, Premier.*

The trip to Honolulu took ten days and the weather was absolutely boiling. We passed Pago Pago, Samoa but due to someone on board having measles, no one was allowed to get off.

CHAPTER 16
HONOLULU TO MANILA:
OCTOBER-DECEMBER 1941

From my diary:

Arrived Honolulu Wednesday, 29ᵗʰ October, 1941. Met by Chinese Consul General Mui King Chau. Took long time at customs as every baggage and package was opened. Lunch with Timperley [H.J. Timperley, an Australian journalist] *and leading Chinese here. Met Mr. Henry Inn who took our photo.*

30ᵗʰ October, 1941. Went at 9:30 a.m. for drive to Diamond Head, Punch Bowl and the Pali. Visited the beautiful home of Mrs. Spalding (formerly house belonged to her mother Mrs. Cooke). Lunch at Lau Yee Chai. Back to Halekulani Hotel. Mr. D had a swim (we also swam yesterday). Went to see The Devil and Miss Jones *at the Waikiki Theatre in evening. Had a front page picture of W.H.D. and me in morning papers.*

Saturday, 31ˢᵗ October, 1941. I love this hotel, the Halekulani. The trees and grass meet the water's edge. We watched the sun sink into the horizon hoping for that emerald flash to appear.

From left: Mui King Chau, Chinese Consul General, W.H. Donald,
Ansie and H.J. Timperley, Australian journalist
Honolulu 1941

Yesterday went to Dr. Chang the dentist. Took trolley car back to hotel for lunch and have just returned from dinner at the Royal Hawaiian Hotel with Mr. K. C. Li and Mr. Mui King Chau. Mr. D and Mr. Li met for first time and they are having heart to heart talks about the whole situation in China.

9th November, 1941, Sunday. The Mui girls (Mook-lan, Sophie and Rosaline, twins) and Mr. Mui came at 3 p.m. to swim. I went with them and their mother to a good Chinese restaurant (Mook Lan Chuen) and later visited Mrs. Chan Hoon and family.

10th November, 1941, Honolulu. Started hula lessons on 8th November (6 lessons ¾-hr for $12) at Betty Lei's, near this hotel. First lesson learned the whole dance of "Liliu". Helen (teacher) says remarkable.

Mr. Mui and Don at the Halekulani Hotel
Honolulu 1941

Dr. and Mrs. Dick Lam took us to see football match, my first American game. Very enjoyable. Later the same day went to a buffet supper at Mr. & Mrs. Sam Young's house (large) where there were about fifty people. Mr. Donald talked for 1-½ hours and answered questions after. Then a short movie and bed by midnight.

Sent wire today to Hong Kong. (Bond, Pan-Am) and also Washington to get seats on Clipper. There was only one steamer with accommodation for one (a makeshift one at that). Today, looks like war with Japan. Churchill says will declare war on Japan one hour after America is involved in any conflict with them.

Honolulu, 14th November, 1941, Friday. What a rush! Heard at 9 a.m. that we could take a look at a freighter, the Don Jose *and decide whether we could stand a trip to Manila on her. We took the* *only two cabins. Paid fare US $250 + 5% tax + customs fees, about $140 totaling $680 for the two of us. Heard trip would take one month to Manila.* [Though we are trying to get to Hong Kong!] *Well stocked up with new books, magazines, two cases each of oranges and apples, biscuits and one jar of marmalade.*

Dr. D. Y. Chang finished fixing my teeth this morning, and I rushed through packing and lunching at the Halekulani. Saw no one except Mrs. Chan Hoon who gave each of us a Shavers Desk set. The Chinese Consul came to see us off.

8:30 p.m. On board freighter Don Jose. *Am going to bed. Have sore throat and catching a cold, and we are still anchored in the harbour. Honolulu pretty at night. Thoroughly enjoyed my seventeen days stay. Bought while in Honolulu: six pairs nylon silk stockings @ $1.65, ten pairs silk stockings @ $1.15-$1.35, four handbags about $2.30 (sent one to Mrs. Furlong), three pairs shoes @ $2.30.*

This ship has a Filipino crew and Captain.

22nd November, 1941, Saturday. Crossed International Dateline and equator. Missed one Sunday (23rd November). So far we have been traveling for seven days without seeing any land. Decks too sunny to sit and dining room too hot. The Captain, Mrs. Remedios, Sparks [the radio officer] *and Chief Officer playing mahjong all day long. Captain is A. Lopez. Bright moonlit nights. We sleep on deck.*

News: looks like war. Karusu's talks with Washington no result. There is part of Japan's navy off Borneo (on our tracks). All leave for soldiers stopped in Singapore and Hong Kong. All must go back to camp immediately. Am reading Out of the Night *by Jan Veltin.*

2nd December, 1941. Today we will pass Port Moresby (New Guinea) but will not go near. Pilot coming out to take us through

*Torres Straits. Hot following winds – 90 degrees in dining room!
Not sick once. Seas very calm and ship heavily laden with battle
equipment for the Canadian troops who were sent to Hong Kong to
help repel the Japanese poised to attack.*

*4th December, 1941. Offshore Thursday Island, Torres Straits,
Australia. Took on pilot at Port Moresby at 10:30 p.m. on 2nd Dec.
He is getting off here this afternoon. I am getting more and more
sun-burnt and will be quite black by the time I get home. Only 9
more days to Manila. Yesterday* Empress of Canada *and convoy
crossed us. Today two large steamers passed us. Mr. D sent letters
off via pilot to the islands and New Zealand. Other letters will be
posted in Manila.*

*6th December, 1941. 7:30 a.m. Sparks told us he just heard that
the Japanese attacked Pearl Harbor and that one Dutch boat was
sunk. Golly, we are right in a death trap. We have passed New
Guinea and getting towards the Celebes. We are passing Amboina,
Indonesia (1,292 miles from Manila). Captain says we'll continue
on to Manila. This latter place has also just been bombed. Japan
has declared war on both America and Britain. We have been
doing about 10-½ knots. Now we'll speed up to 12-½.*

*This morning a steamer is being bombed just north of us, right
on our route between Celebes and Mindanao.* [Heard later they
were looking for us as the weapons for the Canadians had been
loaded from an N.Y.K. (Japanese !) wharf in Canada.]

*11th December, 1941, 8 a.m. Samboanga, Philippines. War
news very bad. Yesterday (10th December), two famous British
warships, the* Prince of Wales *and the* Repulse, *sunk in Singapore.
They also sunk one American battleship,* Oklahoma. *Yesterday, we
passed the very spot where the Japanese were trying to bomb the
freighter* Admiral Cole *a couple of days ago. Japanese trying to*

take Hong Kong by land and also blockading her. Manila now bombed several times.

13th December, 1941, Manila Harbor. At 12:30 p.m., our ship stopped near the entrance of the breakwaters of Manila Harbor.

12:35 p.m., I was on port boat deck when I saw two squadrons (eight each) of bombers fly towards us; they were quite low. I went up to the Captain's cabin to tell him and Mr. D., both of whom were quite unaware of the planes. The radio was on for the news. Mr. D looked at them through field glasses and said, "Japanese bombers".

The women and children were all hurried into the saloon, and in a few minutes the bombers passed overhead. I went to my cabin to get my camera and took three photos of the blaze of smoke coming from the bombed airfield. Then again appearing through the clouds (rainy day) came three more squadrons of bombers and bombed the airfield again. No sirens were heard, no fighters were seen, and the anti-aircraft firing was wide of their targets. At 1 p.m., a half-hour later, all were gone and only the low hum could be heard with a few bursts of machine guns. Everyone on board was furious with our defense.

19th December, 1941, Manila. We [Don and I and the Remedios family from Hong Kong, Tony, Mamie and their three children] *are moving out to San Francisco Del Monte Ave, Quezon City today to a house, having stayed at Avenue Hotel since the 14th (Sunday). The day we disembarked, 13th December, we slept on the verandah of Dr. Lopez's house (the Captain's brother).*

Just bare floors. I did not have a mat or towel under me and it was a most surprising shock to feel so bereft of any bare necessities. But it was kind of our host to take us in.

Within the twenty-four hours of being in Manila there were four air raid alarms. It's hot here. I have bought foodstuffs worth pesos 200 (about HK$400) and 12 tins kerosene for pesos 52.

Boxing Day, 26ᵗʰ December, 1941. San Francisco Del Monte Ave. Opposite X-otic Films, where our house stands. Today Manila has been declared an Open City. All morning the J bombers have been zooming overhead. Two enormous columns of smoke were seen this morning from the back of the house.

Yesterday (Christmas day), the Remedios children, Benita, Antonia and Peter, got up at daybreak and were so excited with their stockings. I cooked Spanish rice and chicken for our Christmas lunch, followed by plum pudding (bought). Cookies and ice cream for tea. (We have no cook, so I am it.) I wouldn't be surprised if Mamie did not know how to boil water, which is not an insult, as that is the way we were brought up in Hong Kong. Mamie gave me some lovely things: a house gown, a velvet apron frock and a green leather handbag. Mr. D gave me (on the 24th) a gramophone and a book. While eating our Christmas lunch the bombers were heard overhead.

1942

1ˢᵗ January, 1942, Thursday. Mrs. B. rang up to say J's will be here in the evening.

2ⁿᵈ January, 1942. Mr. D went to town in morning. He was soon back, riding in one of those absurd looking half-station wagons. He paid four pesos (HK$8) for the ten miles. He found the city full of people running wildly about and saw blazes of fire everywhere. The J's are here today. Mr. D packed a suitcase ready to be sent away to concentration camp. At the side and back of the house can be seen thick black smoke rising out of the city of Manila.

Last Sunday or Monday, our ship the Don Jose *was bombed four times. From 9 a.m. to 3 p.m. waves of bombers harassed the crew. All but one was saved. They had three life boats left and rowed under machine-gun fire to Corregidor, a half mile away. There they were refused food for two days, after which they came back in a tugboat to Manila. Sparks and 2nd officer visited us to tell us about it. We are all waiting for something to happen. It's so quiet you can hear the hens fussing around.*

CHAPTER 17
SULPHUR SPRINGS
INTERNMENT CAMP:
JANUARY 1942

On the evening of January 2nd, 1942, the day Don went into Manila to see if he could find out what was happening, the Japanese army entered the city. There were immediate orders from the radio stations and blaring loudspeakers that all Allied nationals must assemble in various places and bring with them enough personal items to last them a few days. The collection stations were Bay View Hotel, Rizal Stadium, Villamor Hall and Sulphur Springs. The last place was a stone's throw away from our rented house. Sulphur Springs was a modest spa owned and run by a German, Mr. Dahlen. Don walked over there to register, carrying a small bag of clothes with him. He did not return.

Two days later, a small Japanese soldier came to our house holding my passport in his hand, pointed at my picture and said I was to go <u>now</u> with him to camp. Though I had steeled myself against what was taking place, I was thunder struck. Why would they want a Chinese girl to be interned? There were so many

Chinese in the Philippines. No doubt they just looked at my British passport and didn't bother with the photo inside. Don must have taken my passport with him when he went to register at Sulphur Springs.

I ran into Tony Remedios's room to say good-bye. He was thin and wan. I hugged the three darling kids, who sensed something was horribly wrong. Little Peter clung to my skirt. I told Mamie not to cut the pork pie that was baking in a bread tin until it was cold. Outside the house, Mr. Dahlen, now the Commandant of the Japanese internment camp, was waiting for me in a wagon.

From my diary:

6th January, 1942. Surprise! I am now in the Sulphur Springs Camp. Mr. Dahlen came in a station wagon and I was whisked off, just like that! I was in the kitchen making some cookies for W.H.D. to take to him. Good thing I packed one small suitcase this morning. Mamie said, "Why are you packing?" and I answered, "Just in case."

We had lunch here. It was wet rice with chopped pai tsai (Chinese cabbage) and bits of meat. Tea without sugar but with milk. Mamie sent along a hatbox full of sheets and pillow slips and half a pork pie that I had made (not bad) and a tin of biscuits.

The Japanese had turned this spa into a holding zone for the refugees who had come down on the last evacuation ship from Shanghai, the SS *Anhui*. It remained a concentration camp for the duration of the war. The camp's population at this time totaled nine men, a hundred women and a few children. There were two or three English families, and the rest were White Russian wives of Britishers who worked in China. The White Russian women were a jolly, carefree, noisy bunch and all of them spoke some English with heavy accents and were very friendly. They were British by marriage and were being evacuated to Australia when their ship was stopped at Manila.

Sulphur Springs' main feature was its Olympic-sized pool, with a loudspeaker at one end blaring music. The late 1930's dance tunes would have been pleasant under different circumstances. I was given a cubicle in a row of tiny rooms connected by a long corridor on the upper floor of one of several buildings. Don lived in a wooden house, also two floors high, which stood near the wall that surrounded the whole area. But the wall was not too tall for Mamie to throw over packages of precious foodstuff for us. There were no guards that I ever saw, and we could exchange messages at the gate. Soon the Remedios family ran out of money, but Don helped them.

Where were our captors, the Japanese? The German, Dahlen, seemed to be in sole charge.

From my diary:

24ᵗʰ January, 1942, Sulphur Springs Internment Camp. Have been in this British refugee camp twenty days now. Am growing fat! For breakfast (8 a.m.) we eat cracked wheat mixed with a little sugar and a little cocoa, a glass of tea (just like dishwater) and now and then we get hot cakes and a teaspoon of jam instead of the cracked wheat. Twice we have had an egg! For lunch at noon we have cracked wheat mush with a tiny bit of beef stew and a few string beans (including the strings), and tea. For supper we have the same cracked wheat as breakfast. So now I have stopped taking the Vitamin B1 pills and am taking Haliver oil pills containing 8,500 international units Vitamin A. Mamie sends us bread and fruit very often, bless her, and since yesterday I have started to make Lipton's tea over at the wooden shack.

The weather is quite nice now, hot under the sun but chilly in the early mornings. Some of us get up at 6 a.m. and wait in line for some coffee. I have a good mind to cut that out and go over to Don's house and make some for myself. But first I must get Mamie to buy me coffee. I feel healthy and keep myself busy reading and have made some good friends, one of whom is Ida Cunningham.

Don has to go on duty five times in two days. Two hour watch at gate in daytime and round the grounds at night. I serve table (two servers to a table of about twenty) one day every five days. Beginning in a few days, general mopping up and cleaning once a week. I get up at 6 a.m. and go to bed round 9 p.m. After lunch I rest till 3 p.m. then take a shower.

4ᵗʰ February, 1942. This afternoon. moved into a tiny space in the same wood building as Don. The Cunningham family of four is also moving there.

15ᵗʰ February, 1942. Chinese New Year. Singapore fell.

Wednesday, 18th February, 1942. Last Sunday, 15th February was Chinese New Year. Mamie Remedios sent a coffee cake with icing. My goodness, how I enjoyed the sight of it. It was half a cake because, as she explained at the camp gate, the kiddies asked for a slice each. For supper had the most glorious feed: four ham sandwiches each (Don, too, of course), fruit salad, custard that I made (the others had this too) and a piece of the cake. I could hardly stand.

Without any warning, groups of Japanese soldiers would appear in our midst. One frightening night they came upstairs to look at our quarters, and since I did not want to meet them face-to-face I decided to pretend to be asleep in my cubicle. It was after 9 p.m. and already dark. I didn't want them to see my Chinese face. Luckily they were not too drunk, but they did open my door, looked in and continued tramping down the hall, laughing and talking in loud voices. I was frightened.

19th February, 1942. This evening heard we had to move to Santo Tomas Internment Camp in Manila by 3 p.m. tomorrow.

This was my last entry in this diary.

Three years and one month later, after liberation on March 11, 1945, my diaries were returned to me at New Bilibid Prison, Muntinlupa, Luzon, Philippines. This and a half dozen snapshots were all that was left of my luggage. Mr. Dahlen had saved my diaries and Don's papers and returned them to him.

CHAPTER 18
ARRIVAL AT SANTO TOMAS CAMP:
FEBRUARY 1942

Let me pause here and not hurry into a real prison camp. Sometimes when someone asks me what college I went to, I say with a straight face, "The University of Santo Tomas—it's much older than Harvard, being founded in 1611—in Manila." If this doesn't stop them short and they continue, "What school?" you can guess my answer: "The school of hard knocks!"

The main building of Santo Tomas University is very broad and imposing, with three high stories topped by a large clock that chimes out the hours even through the night. More rooms are set further back on the roof, and from here rises a solid tower and above that a cross, so the height makes a good balance for its width. At the entrance of the building is a bronze plaque inscribed with important dates of the "Royal and Pontifical University of Santo Tomas." The founder was The Most Reverend Miguel de Benavides, Order of Preachers, Archbishop of Manila.

In late December, 1941, after a year of concern over the state of unpreparedness for eventual hostilities, Frederic H. Stevens and other businessmen in Manila decided to ask the authorities if the University could be used as a place of internment if it became necessary. The Holy Fathers readily agreed and a written authorization was handed to the Commander of the Japanese forces by a representative of the U.S. High Commissioner when they entered Manila.

Sometime before, the nearly 6,000 students and more than 300 professors at the University departed, leaving the place to be used as a motor pool by the transportation unit of the U.S. Army. They departed hurriedly and other groups also occupied it, but whoever used it last left it in a filthy state.

On January 4, 1942, Santo Tomas had 300 internees. The population exploded as Japanese soldiers rounded up and trucked enemy aliens from the holding sites. In another two days there were 2,000 men, women and children and about ten days later the numbers increased to 3,300. The main building, annex and gymnasium were used to house them. Men and women were separated into different rooms (former classrooms), and mothers with children lived in the annex.

Santo Tomas had been functioning for over a month and a half when those of us in the Sulphur Springs Internment Camp were transferred. Already in place was an Executive Committee and an Advisory Committee, with sixteen department heads of Medical Services, Sanitation and Health, Work Assignment, Education, Library, Vegetable Garden, Religious Services, Public Relations, etc.

Everyone had to be elected by the Internees except the Chairman, Earl Carroll, who at the time of the fall of Manila was the Chairman for the American Red Cross Emergency Committee for the Malate District of Manila. Carroll wrote, "Japanese officials approached me and stated that they wanted me to become the General Chairman of the internees for the purpose of setting up an organization and appointing leaders for each room."

The room leaders became known as "monitors," and the occupants of each room elected them. They had the important job of conducting the roll call and reporting attendance, seeing that rules were obeyed and recommending supplies to be given by the Red Cross to those in need of a bed, clothing, etc. The monitors were the ones to ask the committee to get permission from the Japanese Commandant for an internee's release from camp (illness or other reasons) or transfer to another room.

Of course the head of Santo Tomas Internment Camp was the Japanese Commandant. At the beginning of camp, he and his staff let us rule ourselves and we hardly ever saw any Japanese except for occasional inspection trips by officers or military police when they toured the camp. All business was conducted through our Central Committee.

The Japanese provided nothing for the internees, not even food. Attached to the entrance of the main building was this statement confronting the hordes of the new arrivals:

INTERNEES IN THIS CAMP SHALL BE
RESPONSIBLE FOR FEEDING THEMSELVES.

How were they supposed to do this? Some had brought food with them to last two or three days, and as they were not allowed to go outside, nor had facilities for cooking, the whole idea was absurd and cruel. This ghastly situation brought immediate action from the Chairman of the Philippine Red Cross (American National Red Cross), Thomas J. Wolf, who was, of course, one of the internees. He and other Red Cross officials in the camp soon managed to organize ways and means to provide food for the more than 3,000 souls, and essentials such as beds, clothing, medical supplies, etc. Cooking equipment was brought in, but plead as we might, the Japanese refused to allow any field kitchens into the camp. So internees had to use the former University canteen, and organized a second kitchen at the annex where the mothers and children were housed. A few days later a third kitchen was started at the camp hospital.

The camp had a daily paper called *INTERNEWS*. It was started by Russell Brines of the Associated Press, and it did not seem to have any censorship. Everything that was going on in the camp was reported, except what we really thought of our captors.

There was news of our arrival:

> INTERNEWS, Saturday, February 21, 1942:
> 113 Britons arrive; 'Protective Custody.'
>
> One hundred thirteen British men, women and children arrived yesterday from Sulphur Springs, San Francisco Del Monte, where they had remained in a separate internment camp. They reached Manila shortly after war's outbreak aboard the SS *Anhui*, a British evacuation ship from Shanghai, and were at Sulphur Springs for the occupation.
>
> Camp population last night was 3,324, less than the 3,348 peak of January 25. Meanwhile, the new commandant, R. Tsurumi, assured Executive Committee men in a February 18 interview that camp residents were under "protective custody" and were not prisoners of war or internees. He added no written

regulations were available for governing persons under this status but said he would undertake to prepare a list.

Pending such a list, misdemeanors will be handled as they arise, he said.

Again on February 24, 1942, INTERNEWS continued:

Life at Sulphur Springs was more like a "hotel," but some of the 113 British internees recently transferred here say they are glad to be in "the center of things" at Sto. Tomas.

Brought here last Thursday from San Francisco Del Monte, the arrivals said they were most impressed by the self-government, division of labor and industriousness of Sto. Tomas internees and the camp's cleanliness. Many of the women said they were amazed to see how hard the men work.

At Sulphur Springs each family had its own room; there were no waiting lines. The proprietor and his family cooked food furnished by the Red Cross and British Civil Emergency Committee, and even washed the dishes. There were no Japanese sentries. Internee men alternated in guarding the gate, mostly against looters. Blackout was observed after 9 p.m.

When I arrived at Santo Tomas, I was assigned to a room with the Russian women who did not have any children. I remember only one washroom for our floor and makeshift showers with a few toilets, so there was always a long line. In the living quarters, formerly class rooms, there was barely enough space for the camp cots we bought from the camp store. Under the cots all our possessions would be stuffed in boxes. In the tiny area between the cots, people would struggle to dress and comb hair and be presentable for the new day.

What made me almost sick was that every day we took our cots into the halls to bang them hard down onto the floor so that the bedbugs would get jarred out of their hiding places. Then we squashed them. Horrors, they left bloody spots—our blood! How can such a small bug have such a big thirst? You would never guess what they smell like—essence of almonds. They were everywhere.

One day, a fellow said we had bedbugs in our belts. What a disgusting idea. We laughed at such an absurd accusation. He then told one of our friends to take off his belt, then to knock the buckle on top of the table. Out dropped two bedbugs!

I did not dare write a diary for about ten months (it was forbidden), but made notes. In November of the first year, I obtained a Bureau of Education student note book and anything appearing here in italics is from that dog-eared diary. Nothing was ever written about our captors or news of the war.

The following diary entries were written in November, 1942 about our arrival earlier that year:

20th February, 1942. Driven in buses to Santo Tomas Internment Camp, in Manila. First impressions were quite surprising ones. Enormous circus tent over dining tables gave the effect of a fair. My heart sank when I saw what was to be my sleeping space. One small room, No. 52A, had to take thirty-two of us. Mattresses allotted to us were double ones and there were no beds. Wires were strung haphazardly across the room for our mosquito nets (thousands of mosquitoes). If we wanted to move in or out of the room at night, we had to walk doubled up and try not to step on anyone's toes, or face. The weight of the nets pulled the wires down.

Ansie's diary of Santo Tomas 1942

I was not with Don when Japanese-driven trucks took all one hundred and thirteen of us from Sulphur Springs to Santo Tomas. My mind has blanked out about how we were processed, and of course I did not write down anything in my diary about this. To my relief we soon contacted each other. He told me he wrote his own name, "William Donald," when he registered, for, he said, "I'd feel like a damn fool if they caught me hiding under an assumed name." We thank our lucky stars that the Japanese never did find Don.

Some time later, at a speech in Chungking, a Chinese dignitary mentioned W. H. Donald was in Manila, whereupon the Japanese military came to look for him at Santo Tomas. After finding "William Donald, born 1875" (the correct year of his birth) in the roster of internees, the officer went away saying he was looking for a much younger man. The Committee alerted Don, who told me what had happened.

I went into a funk and prayed earnestly for God to help us. Since Don was an agnostic, I knew he wouldn't be praying. As the days passed, we grew tired of fearing, and we continued to stand in the lines and let ourselves get caught up with mundane worries. However, it's a miracle that some desperate internee did not turn Don in to curry favor or, later, to get more food to save his own life. But, as Margaret Sams says in her book about her experiences at Santo Tomas, *Forbidden Family*[21], she had never heard of W. H. Donald. Since we were in the Philippines, and because of Don's lifetime aversion to publicity, his name was far from a household word in this part of the world.

We later learned that just five days prior to our arrival, three internees caught escaping over the camp walls were executed by firing squad.

The minutes of our camp's Executive Committee of February 13, 1942, stated that three men escaped from the camp by scaling the wall after roll call at about 8 p.m. on Saturday, February 12. They were caught by the Japanese military some five miles north of the camp and brought back to Santo Tomas the next morning. The three were beaten to a point of insensibility; they asked that

---

[21] Margaret Sams, *Forbidden Family, A Wartime Memoir of the Philippines, 1941-1945*, ed. Lynn Z. Bloom (Madison, Wisconsin: University of Wisconsin Press, 1989).

the following message be given to the other internees: "We deeply regret our actions. We know that we made a mistake, and we urge that no one ever attempt it again."

It was not to end there. Although every overture was made to the Japanese High Command by Bishop Binstead, who had lived for many years in Japan and knew several of the Japanese military authorities in Manila, as well as the German Consul and other well-known German residents, there was to be no clemency. A Japanese military court martial in Manila sentenced the three men to death for attempting to escape from the camp.

At 11:00 a.m. on Sunday, February 15, 1942, Messrs. Laycock, Weeks and Fletcher were blindfolded and made to sit with their legs dangling over the grave. Three Japanese soldiers fired at them from fifteen feet. All three collapsed after the first shot; Mr. Carroll counted thirteen bullets. The Rev. Griffiths read the burial service.

On the first page of my diary in Santo Tomas I copied the last stanza from Matthew Arnold's famous poem *Dover Beach*, as it seemed appropriate:

The world which seems
To lie before us like a land of dreams,
So various, so beautiful, so new
Hath really neither joy, nor love, nor light,
Nor certitude, nor peace, no help for pain
And we are here as on a darkling plain
Swept with confused alarms of struggle and flight
Where ignorant armies clash by night.

CHAPTER 19
LIFE IN "SHANTY TOWN"
SANTO TOMAS: 1942

There was much empty space on the University grounds and out of desperation internees eventually filled it with shacks, lean-tos, and shanties. There were strict rules, the main one being that the structures had to be open on two sides, and had to be vacated by 7:30 p.m. The reason for this was that the Japanese did not want internees engaging in "hanky panky" and producing babies in the overcrowded camp. In January of the following year, 1943, four men were sentenced to thirty days in the camp jail as their wives were pregnant. By the autumn of 1944, however, married couples were finally allowed to move out of the buildings and live in their shanties.

One morning I was at the back of the Main Building when a big load of new lumber was being piled on the ground. The Red Cross had brought it in for us to purchase. A few internees were building small shanties, so without another thought I proceeded to buy some too. It would save our sanity to be away from the hundreds of bodies and resounding noise of the wooden *bakyas* (clogs) we wore, and the never-ending greetings and complaining and the ceaseless rounds of "Have you heard ..." rumors.

One of the internees unloading the 2 x 4's told me what to buy. Nearby three young British sailors (they had missed their ship) asked me what I was going to do with the timber. "I am going to build a shanty," I replied. The three got into a fit of laughter picturing this small skinny me, with two short pigtails behind my ears, trying to hammer nails and saw wood. It ended up—you guessed it—with the lads building us a spacious shanty in Shanty Town. It was my first architectural triumph, as the sailors followed my measurements. I plied them with chocolates, which at that time could be bought in the camp store. I later realized that they would rather have cigarettes, so I switched.

Don found a plot for our daytime home just three shanties away from the main path, near the Fathers' Garden in Shanty Town, as this piece of land was named. Going to the food line was not too far a walk.

Our shanty had *sawali* (matting) sides and part of a very colorful piece of canvas that was formerly used to advertise a cowboy movie. To obey the rules for outside visibility we swung the front wall up to form an extra shaded area. This *sawali* "wall" was nailed onto light wood strips, one side hanging from the roof with bent nails and metal hoops or whatever we could buy. Stout supports kept this roof/wall up. The other moveable wall was swung, not from the roof but from one of the main uprights so that when partially open it gave ventilation for the smoke from our cooking contraptions. The whole shanty could be shut up when a typhoon hit. The roof was thatched nipa palm which sloped to the back, and kept the rain out.

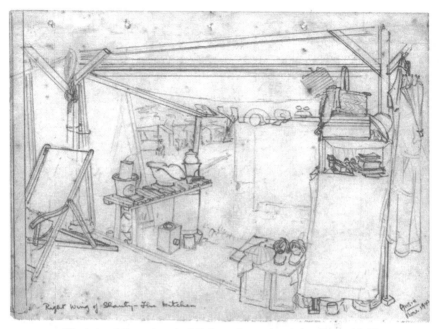

Sketch of the shanty kitchen from Ansie's diary 1942

Miss Berkin, an old China missionary from Kuling (a hill resort near Hankow, China) whom we did not know, had a shack next to ours. She said the lads were glad to have some hard physical work to do.

While these fine sailors were finishing the shanty, I had a busy time "furnishing" it. I bought more wood and had the lads knock up some shelves for the back wall of the shanty. Under the slanted *sawali* roof, there was room for Don's canvas lounge chair, which took up lots of space but was worth it. Near the front left corner was a charcoal burner. Though it looked like any ordinary burner, it could do magic for me. There were a couple of stools and a homemade (by me) cabinet.

At that time we had not met "Chum" Hughes (Allen John Hughes), an Australian who would have scrounged or made all we needed. Chum was an electrician, but he could do anything: build you a palace or mend your delicate Swiss watch. We remained close friends after the war. Dear Chum and his American workmate of the same height and broad build grew beards (both black) and looked like the Smith brothers on the cough medicine bottles. They were so good at fixing electric works that the Japanese would send them on outside jobs. That was when they stole whatever they could lay their hands on for camp needs and for friends.

Back to my yellow student notebook:

23rd February, 1942. Started on morning duties [then quite voluntary] *as a vegetable girl. Cleaned rice, peeled sweet potatoes (horrid job), cut up pai tsai* [a Chinese green vegetable] *scraped carrots, etc.*

The rice and cornmeal were always full of weevils and worms, and I hated the thought of them, much less actually touching them. If you only knew, Ansie my dear girl, that in the months ahead you would be thankful for any solid food and would think that throwing away the sweet potatoes peelings was a mortal sin.

1st March, 1942. Our shanty in Shanty Town nearly completed. We moved in and started a menage of three for meals though Miss. Berkin has hut of her own next door. ["It would look better," she said, as she invited herself in. I suppose she couldn't help being a China missionary trying to save an extra Chinese soul.] *Initial bill for lumber was 19.75 pesos. Labour 10 pesos. Subsequent purchase of* sawali, *etc. made shanty about 50 pesos. At present one can't build shanty for under 100 pesos.*

Many evenings, in the early twilight hour before we left the shanty for the night, three American lads working in Manila would come from the opposite shanty to sit with Don. They were Henry "Hank" Sperry and George Greene, both working for Citibank in

China, and Hal Hertz, Manager of Otis Elevator in Shanghai. Don spun yarns of his former days with the Chinese warlords, the Russo-Japanese war, and the twenty-one secret demands made on the Chinese government by the Japanese.

April, 1942. Landed in camp hospital with enteritis. While there found I had amoebic dysentery. Took emetine injections and enterovioform tablets. Don very energetic.

The doctor wondered why I took it so calmly when he told me I had amoebic dysentery. "Well," I replied, "now that you know what it is, you can cure me." I was so naive about many things. I did not know that in the tropics this type of dysentery is extremely hard to cure, and sometimes the only solution is to send the patient back to England or to the United States or some place with a temperate climate.

I have a pencil drawing of the hospital ward and at the bottom right edge of the picture is a card hanging from the foot of my bed stating, "A. Lee. Acute enteritis April 5." At roll call Carl Mydans came into the ward and called "Ansie Lee" to check me off his list.

9th April, 1942. There was a bad earthquake. Was in hospital and awakened by violent rocking. No damage in camp.

June, 1942. Everyone in Shanty Town preparing for rainy season. Don and I dug ditches around our shanty, raised the floor with earth about 8 inches, put tar paper on roof for which we had to have help.

22nd June, 1942. Don's sixty-seventh birthday. We didn't tell anyone. He insisted on working hard as usual and made a large frame of sawali. It made him very tired.

Ansie's sketch from her hospital bed, Santo Tomas
April 1942

*24th June, 1942. About 11 a.m. Don came back from John
Hunter's* [he had a "restaurant" and sold cooked foods]. *Later told
me Don was sick. Don sat very quietly down on canvas chair and
jokingly said he felt a little dizzy. I continued preparing lunch
without much thought about the matter.*

*At lunch, a seller came and when Don was asked whether he
wanted something or other, to my great astonishment, he could
only open his mouth on his left side and make a few odd sounds. I
sent the seller away and to my horror Don could not even lift his
right hand to his mouth to feed himself. After lunch he rested on his
chair and then I walked with him to his building where he later
saw Dr. Fletcher. During the walk Don could not walk straight but*

gravitated to the right. He had had a stroke and the whole right side of him was momentarily paralysed.

Saw Don through the window and he was sitting up in bed but had not yet seen the doctor. He came back to the shanty with Pop Wright and had supper. He said he felt a little easier and could talk though his mouth, which when he did talk, was crooked. What a dreadful day!

11th July, 1942. Had been feeling more and more run down and finally could not bear it any longer so went to the hospital to see Dr. Robinson. He said at once it was dysentery.

12th July, 1942. I was sent off to St. Luke's hospital (outside camp) where I was given five emetine injections and retention enemas. Dr. Fletcher was my doctor. He told me Don was getting along all right.

I did not know that Dr. L. Z. Fletcher was a highly regarded physician and surgeon in Manila. In camp, he was appointed Medical Director on July 21, 1942, the first year of internment. He not only attended the sick in the camp but he kept regular office hours at Santa Catalina Hospital daily, returning to camp to work in his clinic at the Education Building in the evening. He worked from twelve to fifteen hours a day, seven days a week.

At St. Luke's Hospital, I was placed in a large ward with the beds close together. On one side of me was a Filipino who was dying. I was scared all my waking hours. Death was something eerie. His family looked so mournful and downcast. With not a familiar face in the crowd except Dr. Fletcher, who came twice a day, I was longing for Santo Tomas.

18th July, 1942. After a week I returned to camp to the first flood of the season. In one area I waded up to my knees to the shanty and found Don there trying to kill ants with a hot poker. He had the charcoal stove lighted and was making some tea.

Thousands of red ants were moving up the cupboard and on to the duck boards. The shanty was like a tiny island. He went to the supper line and I ate a lot of red beans, which he brought back. (Note: roughage is like dynamite.) The next day I went back to the camp hospital and stayed there taking my carbarsone pills.

After this period I did not cook for three (Miss Berkin) but made my work as light as possible.

Ants! Of all the infuriating creatures, ants take the cake. There are the normal sized ones as we know them in the civilized world, but not many people have come across ants that are so tiny that you can barely see them. They are so small they can squeeze into your cans of stored food. I have stepped onto a red ant nest and screamed, my whole leg instantly on fire, as hundreds covered my leg and stabbed me with their daggers. In camp every bit of food had to have a moat surrounding it. The water had to be changed often; a layer of dust would suffice as a bridge for the ants to make a quick dash over the water to the food.

The most awe-inspiring sight was during the typhoon season in Shanty Town when our ground was flooded. To save themselves, one clan of ants made a float to drift to higher ground. On closer inspection, I was shocked to see thousands of bodies of their fellow ants sticking together and dying to form this platform.

In recent years my old amah, who was a superb cook, would always tell me when we had ants in the kitchen. But to my amusement, she always whispered when talking about them. To her, ants were a worthy adversary and not to be angered by loose talk.

13th September, 1942. Went into new camp hospital with dengue fever. What a high fever that is! I shake until I am worn out, but cannot stop shaking. My back aches like fury.

20ᵗʰ September, 1942. Since today is my birthday I left hospital yesterday. However, many were the disappointments waiting for me. The chicken which I had ordered (my first time) through George, the bus driver, disappeared from the package line. Don felt awfully sick and had a high fever so he was taken off to hospital. He has dengue fever too! I cooked my lunch so badly I could not eat it. At 3:30 p.m. I went visiting the sick (Don) and then went up to my new room (now 47) to have an early sleep. Dr. Foster Baines gave me a wooden carabao (water buffalo) sculpture.

30ᵗʰ September, 1942. Don stayed ten days and came back to the shanty in a violent typhoon. Just as the poor weak man had settled himself nicely down in his deck chair, in blew one of the walls; then the back sawali *wall gave way. When trying to fix it up, a large piece of lumber hit him right in the middle of his forehead. How lucky it didn't get his glasses and eyes.*

12ᵗʰ October, 1942. Mandarin classes (Mr. George Greene).

I was the pupil and George the teacher. He had quite a large class. I am Cantonese, and did not wish to forget the Peking dialect I learned while visiting Peking in 1935-36. How best to pass the time but to study? Waiting in the long queues whenever there was something for sale, oil for instance, I would take a makeshift stool and study my Chinese homework. After slowly snaking my way through the queue for an hour or more, I might be told the supply of oil or whatever was finished. By studying, at least I didn't waste the time. But it hurt to think how the fates dealt you such a blow.

13ᵗʰ October, 1942. I went to the doctor again as I had the same abdominal pains and cramps. He gave me more enterovioform and more carbarsone (for which I had to pay 8.50 pesos for twenty tablets.) After that another 20 pills of some cheap looking brand for dysentery. Anyway, while taking these I put on several pounds. Am feeling much better.

Don went to *"Ye Olde Bakery"* [run by an enterprising internee who made money during the times when we could purchase flour, eggs and other foodstuff] *and bought two meat pies for 1 peso. We lunched on this at 11:30 a.m. and also had coffee, papaya and some bananas which our shanty neighbor, Mr. Whittall, gave us.*

At siesta hour Mr. George Greene came over so I had to sit up and there wasn't much time left over for sleep as we had planned to go to see the Hobby Show at 2 p.m.

The show was a definite success. The things I liked best were the sketches and printings and especially those of life in this camp; the bamboo steins, carved and sleek looking; the pipes for smokers; the coffee-coloured crocheted bedspread and most of the carved woodwork.

After this show I was fired with enthusiasm to do a little hobbying of my own. Decided I really must start a sketch book so trotted along to the old lady in the ground floor hallway and bought a bottle of paste and a Venus pencil. She had no drawing paper.

20th November, 1942. Don starts on work in big camp vegetable garden.

23rd November, 1942. I land in hospital with acute enteritis. Examination of stool at noon found the elusive amoeba bug. Alas!

30th November, 1942. Writing this in hospital. My day is something like this. Get wakened at six in the morning when night nurse switches on the bright lights. Temperature taken. Wash and breakfast at 7:30.a.m. Eat only half my cornmeal mush, drink a little of my weak and flavourless tea and eat a banana. Doctor does his rounds. Am still on soft diet. Generally feel lazy in the morning, but make myself sit on chair and do my braids. Then open my biscuit tin and choose pencils to either do a little drawing or writing or study Chinese. These things make the hours fly and I forget I am supposed to be sick (but no temperature) and have to stay in hospital. Doze a little before lunch at 12 noon after reading on the bed. Am reading Fanny By Gaslight, *by Michael Sadler.*

Lunch nearly always consists of rice and gravy, a little dessert and tea. Generally go into a sort of drugged trance after lunch and sprawl all over the bed. However, at about 1:30 p.m. when everybody else is having a siesta, I force myself up and have a cold shower. That's always very delightful. Temperature taken and watch other patients beautify themselves for the visitors.

Don comes promptly at 3:30 p.m. and stays till 4:30 p.m. (unless there's something out of the ordinary on the food line when he goes off a little earlier to be under the dining shed before line forms at 4:30 p.m.) Supper at about 5:15 p.m. This is always the same: soup, poached egg on rice, a banana and tea. At 5:30 p.m. I take my chair and go downstairs onto the front lawn. Sit there till the whistle blows at 7 p.m. Don is there with me. Go to see Baker and others in that ward and spend a chatty hour. Wash and go to bed just before lights out at 9 p.m. I don't sleep so well but it doesn't really matter.

26th December, 1942. Still in hospital. That makes it a stay of over a month now. If my writing seems a bit wobbly it's because I'm so weak I can't even write with ease.

On the 4th Dec. I started on a course of two pills of 'Paroxyl' per day for my amoebic dysentery. A couple of days later I started to have a temperature of 99.6 degrees. It rose slowly but surely so on the 10th December the pills were stopped. On the night of the 12th December I had such terrible chills that I was sure it was malaria. I shook so that I was in agony with the strain on my muscles. On the 13th December (the day we arrived in Manila last *year) my temperature rose to 104.8 degrees. The doctor was called and he ordered sulfapyradine and aspirin. All this time my only pains were behind my eyes and shooting pains in my head. Also I couldn't curl my legs up without feeling a strange leaden feeling. That night I vomited the pills up and they tasted so horrible that I continued vomiting, so with the racket I made people next morning said how sorry they felt for me. (I also heard what they remarked behind my back!) The next day my fever went down to 102 degrees and <u>very</u> slowly it dropped. Now three weeks later, I have fever in the afternoon and night of 99.6 degrees.*

Yesterday was Christmas day and it was a surprise Christmas for me. I had such a lot of presents I didn't expect. Don gave me a large bottle of cologne, a pair of scissors and a box of sweets. Mr. Cameron sent me a stuffed turkey with all the trimmings, a large Christmas cake, a box of chocolates and flowers and a Christmas card. Unfortunately I felt too excited to eat but some of the patients here had some of the turkey and I gave Mrs. Lester the rest. Don took the cake to his supper party—Mrs. Corfield's, held at our shanty.

Dear Mr. Cameron, I'm sorry I do not remember who you are, but thank you with all my heart for your Christmas gift. In all my life I have never had such a wonderful, unforgettable surprise!

CHAPTER 20
SECOND YEAR AT SANTO TOMAS: 1943

From my diary:

Beginning of the end of our camp life.

The end? What a laugh!

2nd January, 1943. On New Year's Eve, the Filipinos around the camp made a continual noise banging tin cans and other metallic objects. I stayed awake at the camp hospital till the New Year came in. Our big clock struck the hour very ponderously and one man in camp shouted out something that sounded like, "yahoo!" He must have been one of our own guards.

New Year's Day wasn't very different from any other day except for repeated congratulations to the other patients and the nurses. I wished Dr. Stevenson KUNG HEI FAAT CHOY and he said the same. Then, he very enthusiastically described the wonderful Chinese dinner he had the day before, all in the Cantonese dialect!

I am still weak. My temperature is normal in the early morning and stays higher the rest of the day. Don says he feels well but he is thinner. The muscles in my hand are painful from writing this.

Dr. Stevenson was very handsome, well known as a quarter-miler during his Princeton days. He and his twin brother were outstanding students at Princeton and Yale. They grew up in China, of missionary parents, I believe.

3rd January, 1943. Think of it. I am taking five kinds of things to make me well: a liquid tonic, an iron capsule, TWO yeast pills, all three times a day; 20 mg vitamin B1 injections every other day, and a dose of clear cod-liver oil every morning. I am on a full diet and also an eggnog in the morning and calamansi [Filipino lime] juice at 3 p.m. Yesterday I started to feel hungry even after my meals! Great improvement.

I am so grateful for all those who were caring for me: Don, who came to cheer me up every day, and the doctors who must have given orders for these extra rations. I always had the highest regard and affection for the doctors: Dr. L. Z. Fletcher who kept up my morale when I was at the outside hospital at St. Luke's; kindly Dr. Hugh Robinson who was lucky enough to be repatriated; Dr. T. D. Stevenson with whom I had a happy rapport. Since the latter lived outside camp for the first two years, it's no wonder he had a festive Chinese New Year's dinner. There was Kitty Fairman, the dietician in charge of the hospital food, whom I remember fondly, and every one of the Army and Navy nurses who were real angels and brightened my days. I am alive because of each and every one of you. Thank you all.

10th January, 1943. Am supposed to be leaving hospital tomorrow, but as I still run a small temperature I might not be allowed to go. Tomorrow will be seven full weeks in hospital!

13^(th) January, 1943. Am still in. We are at the moment rather poor and so am glad Don is eating at the hospital. He has only about thirty pesos left.

Yesterday about twenty-five officers and enlisted men in our camp and a few others were taken off in a truck at 3 p.m. to be questioned at Fort Santiago.

The Spaniards in Manila built Fort Santiago in the 16th century. In peacetime the Americans used the buildings as offices and living quarters for the U.S. Army. The Japanese resurrected Fort Santiago's dungeon and here prisoners were herded so tightly that there was not enough room to lie down. Extra detention cells were later built to house the growing number of people dragged in to be questioned.

The *Free Philippines*, published by the U.S. Army Office of War Information after liberation, describes Fort Santiago under the Japanese. From the issue dated March 3, 1945:

> Those in the cells were packed close. At night when a man lay down to sleep he could not move till morning. During the day each sat on his haunches, the Japanese way. He must not talk.
>
> Those who were taken in for questioning were beaten, burned with cigarette butts, slashed or filled with water to almost bursting and then struck a heavy blow in the pit of the stomach. There are other ways, too. One boy, who had been caught operating an underground broadcasting station, tried to escape from the fort to avoid certain execution. He was caught in the attempt, his foot impaled on the floor with a bayonet, and finally his head was cut off.

Each prisoner was taken out of the cell again and again and questioned relentlessly for hours. Every angle was covered by the investigation. If one did not answer well, it might be the last thing he'd ever do.

From the *Free Philippines*, April 4, 1945:

The evidence of these atrocities, resulting in the deaths of some 400 persons, was found in three different places in Fort Santiago. Death had been caused by shooting, bayoneting or starvation. The majority of the bodies had their hands tied behind them.

Bodies were in such a position that a group could have been faced against the wall, and shot in the back. Then another group would be brought in to suffer a like fate, with their bodies falling over those of the first group. The bodies were shrunken, giving evidence of malnutrition and near-starvation.

In the 15 by 18-foot dungeon of Fort Santiago were found some 30 bodies. It was impossible to detect any wounds on the partially decomposed bodies, but there was every indication that they had died of starvation. The dungeon's thick ceiling and walls made it bomb proof, and the inside was not disturbed by any American artillery activity. This fact lends additional weight to the theory that the people were locked in the dungeon and left to starve.

From my diary:

14th January, 1943. Nurses (Army) didn't come on duty at 7 a.m. this morning. On strike! Facts (or rumours) of the affair: that Army Head Nurse Mrs. Davison gave an ultimatum to Mr. Grinnell (Executive Committee) that her nurses would not move to the new room designated for them. If made to do so, they would not work any more at the hospital. Grinnell: "We had nurses before you arrived."

15th January, 1943. Nurses were moved (forcibly) though they appealed to Commandant.

19th January, 1943. Another bombshell. 8 p.m. announcement. Use of all shanties to be discontinued but we were to have twenty-four hours to take things out. Also all pregnant women married or not were to be sent to some place in San José and men involved jailed in room behind Commandant's office where they were to be accorded the least facilities to anything, even exercise (poor devils). Commandant claims we did not follow the rules regarding the use of shanties so he ordered their use immediately forbidden.

A count of the numbers of shanties was 554 and users were 2,030. Added to this were 167 internees spending their days in the courtyards of the Main Building, where they made forty-seven shelters or cabañas. The total number of internees who were away from the interior of the buildings during the day was 2,197, a goodly number to relieve the congestion of the rooms.

20th January, 1943. I was permitted two hours out of the hospital to go to the shanty to see about packing up. However, Don had already done it all.

8 p.m. Announcement. We are allowed a further few hours before vacating shanties—till 2 p.m. tomorrow. Also Commandant wishes to announce that we are all to sit on chairs in the evening.

No sitting or lying on the grass or otherwise in reclining positions (so that we shall not catch colds, added Miss Adams).

25th January, 1943. My temperature has been normal for four days, so I am going 'home' after lunch.

Four days later on January 29, 1943, internees were allowed to return to their daytime use of the shanties. I was back in our little grass shack happily messing around the clay stoves, which was my medium for making magic changes (often not successfully) to our humdrum food. We used charcoal made from coconut shells, little thin black bits and pieces which, when coaxed to burn with paper and kindling, would turn a deep red and throw out immense heat. I had to keep adding a little bit at a time so as not to waste any, yet enough to do a good job on the food I was cooking.

5th February, 1943, Friday. They say it's Chinese New Year. Don celebrated by going to the hospital with a temperature of 101.4 degrees.

I feel fine. Weight 102 lbs. Had Chinese lesson today. Am on the regular squad for vegetable and rice detail. Don had his food card stamp for noonday meal, so now I don't cook so much. Weather hot again. Air-raid blackouts are forthcoming.

6th February, 1943. Don has amoebic dysentery.

27th February, 1943. I am getting fat! 104 lbs.

A Day in the Life of an Internee:

Got up 6:30 a.m. and was down at the shack at 7 a.m. Don made breakfast for himself, as I had to rush off to do vegetable duty. Before going I washed a skirt, a blouse and a nightgown. For breakfast had an eggnog (made with the Klim from the Canadian Comfort Kit. Klim is milk spelt backwards.)

7:20 -8:50 a.m. Peeled pumpkins.

8:50-9:05 a.m. Stood in line in toilet (10 minutes).

9:05-9:25 a.m. Stood in line to buy meat. Bought a round steak and half dozen eggs. (20 minutes).

9:25-9:40 a.m. Went to Mrs. MacAvoy's shanty to get typewriter to do some typing for her.

9:40-10:00 a.m. Prepared food for our own cooking. Peeled sweet potatoes and sliced meat thinly, cutting out tough parts and pounding them. Received a chit from Hospital saying Dr. Stevenson wanted to see me. Now I won't be able to get in a full hour of typing.

10-11 a.m. Bought one loaf bread and walked over to hospital. Met Don on the way and he came with me. Doctor only wanted to know how I am and that I was not to go on vegetable detail anymore (I think they are getting all old amoebic dysentery cases out of food handling jobs.)

11-12:30 p.m. Prepared lunch. Ate fried steak and tomatoes, mashed potatoes, bread and jam, cocoa (off chow line).

12:50-1:50 p.m. Came upstairs, third floor to have siesta.

1:50-2:50 p.m. Ironed clothes in corridor with electric iron.

3-3:40 p.m. Had a shower and changed into slacks suit. Went down to shanty.

3:40-4:35 p.m. Typed for Mrs. MacAvoy's next lecture on Peter the Great and the Russian Church.

4:35-5 p.m. Ate meat loaf, squash, rice and tea for supper. Very good. Don was on the line for 20 minutes!

5-6 p.m. Typed again.

6-6:40 p.m. Saw softball game (latter half) 'Phillies' and 'Reds'.

I often watched the internees play softball. Playing first base was Henry Sperry, known as "Hank," a tall, lean and very lanky American, shirtless, catching the ball nonchalantly. When needed he would, in a split second, throw that ball to second base for a double play with loud shouts of approval from the sidelines. I had been partial to tall, lanky men since seeing my first Gary Cooper movie in Marseilles in 1928. When I met Henry, I almost expected him to speak like my film idol. Luckily he did not, as Gary Cooper's hesitant, shy way would not do at all for the New York banker that Henry was. I wonder if Gary Cooper had anything to do with my marrying that first baseman?

6:40 -7:30 p.m. Sat on the road in front of Main Building waiting for the staging of the Radio Show. Sewed my new flared skirt which I am making from a bed sheet.

7:30-8:45 p.m. Radio Show—excellent entertainment.

8:50-9 p.m. Washed.

9 p.m. Roll call.

All that bowing to the Japanese guards while on roll call, and stopping (and bowing) when you were unlucky enough to bump into a guard. A tirade and a hearty slap in the face if you were slow to comply.

And here I am writing. In a short while the lights will go out. Bother! I have brought up my class books to do my Chinese homework. How shall I ever have time. I also want to wash my hair, fix my bakyas, *finish reading* Berlin Diary *and get on with* Well's History. *No time for anything these days.*

4th February, 1943. Was told last week not to work on vegetable detail (amoebic), so today started to go with Don to a shanty where they do book binding. Did 2-¼ hours stripping bindings off old books.

Bookbinding was the best of the work in camp as there were only a few of us. We could chat as we worked, and the internees there were most interesting. There was Margaret Sherk, later Margaret Sams, with her little boy David, Dr. Foster Baine, Don and one or two others.

Don wondered when some big Japanese military general would visit Santo Tomas and recognize him. He knew several of them. He beat one at a North China golf tournament in Peking while he was living there, many years ago. It was a foreign game to me then and his description of how to hit that little golf ball was comical. "If you were swatting a fly, the best way would be to just hit it and not worry about anything else."

6ᵗʰ April, 1943. I have been put on the Education Department and am typing my Chinese notes for George Greene. Health good, weight 103 lbs. Don is well, weight 165-167 lbs.

I will not bore you with the incessant entries of how much everything had gone up in price: brown sugar, rice and cassava flour, hen and duck eggs, fats, meats, soaps, etc. It was a continual worry, not to mention having to borrow money from someone who had contact with the outside. It was known that the Chinese made loans with no collateral or interest. Even if you had money, you had to stand in line for everything.

When we first entered camp, the Japanese did not provide any food and the Philippine Red Cross (American National Red Cross) fed us. After that, from July 1942 to the end of January 1944, the Japanese provided each internee with 70 centavos daily for the entire operation of the camp: food, medicines, sanitation, construction. The Food and Supplies Department (under the camp's Central Committee) headed by George M. Bridgeford was in charge of supplying food for the camp. Allocated for food was 48 centavos per person. As the months passed, even with some increase in money by the Japanese, prices for foodstuffs soared and the worth of the Japanese money decreased so that the amount left to feed us was about 60% less. By the autumn of 1944, starvation caused many deaths, which increased until liberation came in early 1945.

9ᵗʰ May, 1943. Excitement! This afternoon the military took over the camp and before long rumours were racing around camp. Evening announcement: we are to be moved to Los Baños and that 800 men are to go on Friday (14ᵗʰ May) to build more accommodations. All Japs & Filipinos who had small daytime shops in the camp were given very short notice to leave at about 2:30 p.m. Package line from outside closed till Thursday, the 13ᵗʰ.

The May 9ᵗʰ, 1943, evening broadcast over the loudspeaker was from our Executive Committee conveying to all the internees statements from the Commandant of the camp. The latter was authorized by the Director General of the Japanese Military Administration regarding the change of location of enemy civilians. The broadcast said that since there were 2,000 more enemy nationals to be interned and there was no more space in Santo Tomas, the Military Authorities had decided to move all of us to Los Baños. "On the 14th of this month, 800 men selected from the present internees will be dispatched there by train. It is to be emphasized," continued the broadcast, "that this change of location is entirely based upon humanitarian consideration of your own welfare and that fairness in the treatment to be accorded internees shall always be maintained."

14ᵗʰ May, 1943. 800 men left at 7:30 a.m. for Los Baños. Among them being some friends: old Captain Williams (he volunteered), C. C. Chapman (Chappie) Clifford, his friend George Greene, Hank Sperry, Hal Hertz and Whittall.

Los Baños was part of the University of the Philippines and was the agricultural school, used as an experimental farm. It was south of Manila, on the southern edge of a huge lake, Laguna de Bay.

Soon after the end of the war "Chappie" gave me a copy of his "LOGS" in which he wrote in great detail his daily life during internment. Here is his description of moving from Santo Tomas to Los Baños:

> May 12, 1943. Got my baggage out just before 8 a.m. If 800 internees' baggage covers one acre, the remainder of the 4,000 (or 7,000) will take 14 special trains. Camphor wood chests, filing cabinets, sewing machines, etc., 1,000 tons apparently. I dunno where they will put it. Got my machine, pillow and blanket out so can travel relatively light.
>
> May 14, 1943. "Up betimes" meaning 4:30 a.m. Not feeling too good. Furry tickling sensation in throat. Also, suffering from a disposition soured by a loud speaker named (*name deleted)* where he tended bar before he became a combination Admiral, General I dunno, but he is the most opinionated ass I have heard spouting his mouth until 2 a.m. in the night before one breaks camp for Los Baños.
>
> Will say for the Japs, they took us in trucks from Sto. Tomas to the railroad station. Convenient all around as it took fewer guards. Had baggage inspection at the Station. Not so much with the idea of finding anything to confiscate as to require the internees to open their luggage in the dust. The "Bicol Express" consisted of a large number of steel cars. Ours was No. NBB 652. Side doors. The boys who drew the ends must have had a bad time as the sides of the car were too hot to touch. At first only one door was allowed opened, but before we got out

of Manila entirely, they opened up the other door.
The Japs have quite an airfield and large hangars at
McKinley.

Back to my diary:

*17th May, 1943. Several hundred foreigners are coming into this
camp to be re-interned.*

In China and in Hong Kong, the locals, both the Chinese and
expatriate community, always referred to the English, Americans
and non-Asians as "foreigners." Indians and other Asians were not
grouped as "foreigners."

I met one Chinese woman in the first year of Santo Tomas, but
only once, and I never saw her again. Some Chinese were interned
in other parts of Luzon, but there were so many Chinese whose
homes were in the Philippines, they were soon released.

I read in *Santo Tomas,* by Frederic H. Stevens, of a Chinese-
American, Tun Yun Lee, who interned with us. He was an A.B.
seaman on the *President Grant* and had been stranded in Manila.
In February of 1944 the military ordered us to sign an oath not to
"conspire" against the Japanese Military Forces or to escape from
camp. By October, 1944 everyone had signed except Tun Yun Lee.
He was an American and proud of it and would not sign, so he was
put in jail and there he stayed till the end of the war when the First
Cavalry released him on February 3, 1945.

*15th June, 1943. We are still at Santo Tomas. No one has gone
to Los Baños after the first batch left. The rainy season started at
the beginning of this month.*

*I now have invented a good way of baking and we have roast
beef, muffins, and cakes (on special occasions) as easily as
cooking any other way. I just use a native charcoal stove, put my
hot coals right on the bottom where the ashes are supposed to be,*

and place the baking pan in the bowl of the stove. Then, depending on the size of the cake, a tin washbasin or frying pan, is placed upside down on the rim of the stove. Hot coals are put on top as well so that the things brown beautifully. Cupcakes take 10-15 minutes. For a roast I first sear the meat on an open fire before slowly baking it. This slowness helps to make the tough meat tender. I mix my own flour mixture, viz. 1/3 each of rice, cassava and corn flour. Soured coconut milk and soda give the cakes lightness and brown sugar gives them a better taste than white. A little spice or chopped up fresh ginger takes the dullness away.

In the last three weeks we have had a terrific lot of rain and I was tempted to buy a pair of rubber boots but as they cost 30 pesos ($60 HK), I thought better of it. It's nice and sunny and hot now.

17th August, 1943. Night before last we presented a petition to Miss Beaumont, our room monitor, to make a fairer arrangement of room space. Last night she resigned and Miss Holmes is now our new monitor. Today finished drawing picture of our shanty. Am knitting my first pair of panties. It is very pretty—pink. Now studying the Kuoyu Primer *by R. H. Mathews. (Published China Inland Mission, 1938).*

9th September, 1943. Heard this morning about Italy capitulating. Food situation in camp (and outside) getting worse and worse. On 26th August, 1943, told no more fresh meat will be sold (they are controlling slaughtering of cattle etc.). So we are now on a vegetable and bean diet. Since that date we have only had one beef stew. So far, however, there are chicken, eggs and cold cuts to be had at the Camp Cold Stores. Bread this month was raised to 60 cents a loaf (rice bread). Started French lessons with M. Bonnet on 6th September from 4-5 p.m. in the Fathers' Garden, three times a week. My days are more enjoyable now; still busy but *doing things like drawing and reading; not so much drudgery. Hot fine days. Not nearly as wet as last year.*

Last night a lady did chalk-drawings on a blackboard while Mrs. Hill sang. She did stunt drawings too. It was amusing and different. I went by myself as Don had his usual Wednesday meeting. Last Saturday Dave Harvey gave a minstrel show. Jolly good. Yesterday officially announced that no British were going on the exchange ship which is due here end of this month. The Lesters, Allen, Barbara and Geoff, will go as they are Canadians.

26ᵗʰ September, 1943. A Red Letter Day for 127 internees who left camp at 5:30 a.m. to be repatriated to England or Canada. Their exchange ship, the SS Teia Maru, *awaits them at an undisclosed port. The Commandant refuses any reports of the conditions of the camp to be sent with them.*

29ᵗʰ September, 1943. My 29th birthday last Monday, September 20th. Had the Lester family and Father Timmons over for a farewell tea. I made a large cake, cupcakes and roast beef sandwiches. Bought assorted cakes, some cookies and cut thin slices of bread and buttered them. We so enjoyed it. Wore my white dress with red belt and new scarlet bakyas. *The Los Baños boys who are going on this exchange ship came down on the 20th in George's bus. Among them was George Greene.*

On the 21st Miss Ruth Swanson and Lilius Lester gave me a birthday tea at Lilius' shack.

Yesterday had George in our Shanty for supper. Everything turned out nicely, the lemon meringue pie being a great success. We three went afterwards to a play reading, "First Lady". It was amusing. The weather is fine again now, but very hot in the afternoon.

7ᵗʰ October, 1943. Don filled in ditch in our back garden and planted a few cannas. Heard today independence will be given to the Philippines on the 14th.

Very thrilled with new technique of pencil drawing using a chisel edge.

18ᵗʰ October, 1943. Don and I were not around in Shanty Town when the Commandant and his party inspected our area.

14ᵗʰ November, 1943. Big flood; water up to waist for two days

Many shanties were destroyed by the violent storms. Gas and electricity failed and drinking water had to be boiled as it was contaminated.

Hobby show. Had two sketches in it. The show lasted for four days.

I did a few sketches of camp life, but I gave most of them away. I have seen some of them published in books about Santo Tomas. One internee couple wanted to buy one of my sketches of Santo Tomas's main building with the clock tower. I said no, it wasn't for sale. But several weeks later I just gave it to them. Many years later, I got a package in the mail; it was my sketch with a note from the wife, saying her husband had passed away and she wanted me to have the sketch back.

1ˢᵗ December, 1943. Announcement made that Filipino fruit and vegetable stalls and Jap stalls will be closed. Tomorrow morning we can go marketing at the camp market. Hoorah! Feel sick today, sore throat and touch of fever.

Ansie's sketch of Santo Tomas 1943

17th December, 1943. Received four comfort kits from American Red Cross. I have three invalid packages and one ordinary. Each invalid kit contains:

1 lb. Milko, 3 butter, 2 chopped ham & eggs, 1 Prem, 1 Bovril corned beef, 2 Kup Kafay, 1 salmon, 1 paté, 1 prune, 3 corned pork loaf, 1 grapelade, 2 chocolate, 2 cakes soap, 1 cane sugar, 1 Kraft cheese, 1 packet. bouillon powder.

Christmas Day. 1943. Just had the most lovely lunch with Isla & Gillian Corfield & Doug at our new shanty. Doug roasted a most delicious stuffed turkey and he made coffee ice-cream. There was a wee plum pudding (mine, left over from last Christmas, tinned) with rum poured over. Two cakes (one I made, a fruit cake).

I gave Don a handkerchief (unfinished) which represented about half dozen hankies. I decorated the shanty with branches of a nearby tree which has beautiful yellow flowers. David (5 years old) came down to play with his toys. We are going up to have dinner at 7 p.m. with the Sherks. I am wearing my white dress. Weather during day as hot as ever. Don has a cold and bad cough. He went to hospital for enteritis about ten days ago but came out after four days.

Today, one dessert spoon of sugar was served at breakfast. First time for over a month. No sugar is allowed for sale!

New Year's Eve. Had tea party with the Corfields and 'Pop' Wright.

CHAPTER 21
LOS BAÑOS CAMP:
1944-1945

In the spring of 1944, with more internees arriving at Santo Tomas, we were told that we could choose to move to Los Baños. We were moved by truck.

Here is a description of our arrival from Chappie's journal:

April 7, 1944

Watta day, watta day!! The famous 530 arrived and watta 530. If P.T. Barnum were alive today and knew about the internees that came up today from Sto. Tomas, P.T. would have fired all his freaks and hired almost any ten at random and found he had a much better collection.

The only ones I was interested in were Miss Lee and Don. She arrived in the first contingent and somehow got past me without my seeing her, but Don did not come till the afternoon. Miss Lee was supposed to be in with a Miss Swenson, a missionary gal. But as all things are balled up all the time anyway, she found she was bivouacked with a crooked legged crossed-eyed gal, apparently slightly *kichigai* (Japanese for "crazy") and it took much of the forenoon to get it straightened out. Don did not show up till nearly 5 p.m. and was accommodated in Cottage 8, which is much better for him than anything we could have offered here.

In Los Baños, we were not allowed to roam all over the camp. Besides, as far as I knew, there was just the one road with the barracks strung along it. In Santo Tomas there was a huge campus to visit your friends, go to lectures in the Fathers' Garden, play sports and rub shoulders with hundreds of internees collected together for different study groups. We could also visit while waiting in the lines for food, toilet, and to purchase items for sale. And we would gather for the evening entertainment. I would also spend a lot of time around my charcoal burner when there was enough food to bother to improve its flavor.

Life was completely different in Los Baños. We were all in our barracks with no place to go. I did not bother to write much in my diary.

To relieve the tedium, several of the internees were asked to give lectures on their areas of expertise. Henry Sperry asked me to type up his notes for his lectures on banking. He was also on the work brigade that organized the sale of local fruits and vegetables, when available. I noticed that he would always choose some of the best and bring them to me as a present.

Henry and I started spending more time together. One evening, while attending a musical entertainment (one of the few activities available at Los Baños), we found ourselves holding hands during the concert. It took me by surprise, how all of a sudden I had fallen in love. Although we didn't talk much about it, Henry and I knew that we would be together when the war was over and we were out—whenever that might be.

23ʳᵈ July, 1944, Sunday. Henry picked worms out of my corn flour! Took him from 1:30 p.m. to 4 p.m. Went to Sunday evening concert. Don left in the middle of it. Henry and I held hands.

Our "concerts" consisted of listening to records played over loudspeakers. I still have the small piece of paper, yellowed and torn, on which Henry wrote the music we listened to that night. Dated July 23, 1944, he listed:

1. *Overture "Die Meistersinger," by Wagner*
2. *La Boutique Fantasque, by Rossini*
3. *Piano Concerto No. 1 in E Flat Major, by Liszt*
4. *Arias a) Una Voce Poco Fa, by Rossini* [Barber from Seville]
   b) Polonaise (from Mignon), by [Ambrose] *Thomas*
5. *Symphony No. 3 in C Major, by St. Saens*

As the war went on, the daily food rations were getting smaller and smaller, and we were hungry all the time. We thought of food constantly. One of the major pastimes was imagining in great detail the meals we would eat when we were freed. Even the men started collecting and swapping recipes, just like women! People became weaker and weaker and almost every day people would die of starvation.

1ˢᵗ November, 1944. Expect them any day now. I weigh 98 lbs. Henry 150 lbs. Don keeping fairly well. Line calories, about 800.

Another New Year, now 1945. It came with hope of deliverance, but would it be in time?

THE BIGGEST SURPRISE OF MY WHOLE LIFE!

7ᵗʰ January, 1945. At 4:15 a.m. this morning, we were told YOU ARE FREE. Free? The Japanese gave the Committee a written statement that by 5 a.m. they would leave the camp. Thank God. We have been really starving for months. Was awake for hours by Japanese guards tramping back and forth, and in the early hours, about 3:30 a.m., our monitor was asked for all the spades in the barracks. We have none, he said. I was so curious about it that it kept me wide-awake. Henry came at 5 a.m. Last night he said he expected to be free any moment, strange he should say it. Weight today after a heavy mush breakfast, 93 lbs. Henry weighs 134 lbs. (He is 6'3".)

I made notes in my diary from an official document I read at the time, "Record of the Event of Jan.7, 1945 affecting the Los Baños Internment Camp:"

11:50 p.m. Mr. George Gray of the Administration Committee was asked that every shovel, private and camp-owned, be turned over to the Japanese authorities before 1:00 a.m. Forty-seven were collected. The Commandant's car, the Japanese International truck and the Oldsmobile owned by the camp were all collected in front of the Commandant's office.

3:30 a.m. Messrs. Heichert, Watty, Gray and Downs at conference with the Commandant and Mr. Ito. The Commandant said:

"From now on, internees are released from my charge. By sudden order from our Superiors, I release all internees from 5:00 a.m. in the morning to the Administration Committee. Your committee is given complete charge of the entire camp. We are willing to leave all food provisions that will last for at least two months. I would suggest that your Committee keep all internees inside the camp. By our orders within about one hour we must leave here. This is all I want to tell you."

The Commandant wished the Chairman, the Vice-Chairman and Secretary to sign a list containing the names of all people in the internment camp of this date.

"On this date, January 7, 1945 at 3:45 a.m., I, M. B. Heichert, Chairman, Administration Committee, received the release from the care of the Commandant, Major Iwanaka, of Internees of Philippines Internment Camp #2, Los Baños, P.I."

At 4:45 a.m. they drove off and at 5 a.m. Chairman Heichert broadcast over the loudspeaker that the Japanese had all departed and that we were FREE.

We were all stunned, and overjoyed, and still afraid. It was so hard to believe, like a cruel dream. We laughed and cried and embraced each other. Then the loud speaker summoned us to go in front of Barracks 15.

At sunrise there was a flag raising in front of Barracks 15.

There was a short but moving ceremony with Bishop Binstead giving thanks for our deliverance, a prayer for the dead, the Lord's Prayer and the Blessing. The American flag (so carefully hidden these three years) was unfurled and hoisted up on a bamboo pole and the "Star Spangled Banner" was sung, followed by "God Save the King."

Jerry Sams, who had a radio secreted in his cubicle even though the penalty was death, now brought it out in the open. On the next day, January 8, 1945, we heard Roosevelt's Annual Address to

Congress. The part that I remember was that he asked for more nurses to help the war effort, and I thought to myself, fancy having to plead for this. They must not know how great was the suffering of all those involved in the war.

As soon as some of the internees knew the Japanese barracks were emptied, they rushed in and looted them. This included food, the Commandant's kimono, his bike, his dishes and two radios from the garrison quarters.

We were warned not to go outside the camp as we were still in enemy territory, with a division of Japanese soldiers just over the hill. I did not try to get extra food from the Filipinos outside the fence, as now there was enough to eat on our own food line.

The kitchen staff produced thick mush for our breakfast, two scoops each. We received three meals a day with food that we could actually chew on instead of food that was so watered down, you could drink it. Six days went by, and we were able to cheer our planes as they flew for some bombing mission and go to bed with our tummies full, not quite believing in our present strange situation. Strangely, those who had beriberi, Henry included, did not have their conditions relieved with the extra food. They continued to have puffed up faces in the morning, looking like cherubs.

A Waking Nightmare

It hurts even to write about it. On January 13, 1945, *they* returned in the dark of night. It was 2:30 a.m. Six days of freedom and then it was as if a black pall was flung over the camp to stifle any hope of deliverance.

13th January, 1944. Saturday. About 2 a.m. Konichi, the Commandant and his staff returned!!! I was wakened by a loud *voice in the hall stating that fact at 3 a.m. If ever a nightmare came true that was the time. All of us were astounded and horrified. Only two meals today.*

How we all hated Konichi. There were plenty of coconuts and vegetables growing all around us, but he wanted to watch us starve to death. The location of Los Baños was chosen by the University of the Philippines as their School of Agriculture for its fertile soil. Major Owanaka was the actual commandant, but he left the running of the camp to his underlings, such as Konichi.

The Japanese wanted their radios back—or else. But they did not exist any more. Whoever had swiped them (there were two) had taken them to Jerry Sams to have them fixed. During our Six Days of Freedom, the Committee wanted to have a transmitter so Jerry dismembered the two Japanese radios to get parts for a transmitter and parts needed for his own radio.

Now someone's head had to roll or the whole camp would suffer. There is a whole story concerning this radio in Margaret Sams's book, *Forbidden Family.* Though the incident ended without reprisals, it showed man's inhumanity to man, with Jerry about to be sacrificed. No one came forward with the radios. To save face, a member of the Japanese office force came to the committee and said that *any* radio would be acceptable and the matter would be closed if one was produced. As luck would have it, there was an extra radio that a Filipino had brought in to Jerry to be fixed. With this in a gunny sack, Jerry took it and left it in the Japanese office as soon as night fell. He did not meet any guards.

14th January, 1945. Sunday, 2 p.m. They made us stand in the sun for two hours for roll call. But the roll call was just one of Konichi's tricks. He had soldiers search our barracks. In two of the men's barracks, the internees found out and went in a body to refuse entry to the searchers. The search was called off but half an *hour later a cordon of Japs was put round these two barracks and a thorough search was made <u>but</u> in the presence of the occupants.*

Two men have been shot going out of camp. The second one shot to death by order of the Commandant two hours after he was wounded.

The first, Jan Hell, or "Pat," as he was known, went out frequently after he had made contact with a Filipino during our six days of freedom. He brought in chickens and coconuts and other foods for some of his friends as well. On January 17, 1945 he was shot just outside the fence.

On January 28, 1945, another internee, George Lewis, was shot after he had already climbed back inside the fence and was in the camp. The guard had put a bullet in his shoulder. Dr. Nance tried to reach the bleeding man, but was threatened. George Lewis was left there bleeding for one and a half hours until they finally carried him in and killed him with a shot in the head.

There was no more news as Jerry Sams had no more power for his radio. Dr. Nance and Jerry had a plan. Our friend Chum Hughes had the Commandant's bike and he, Dr. Nance, Jerry, and another man were trying to use the bike to get the generator going. They were caught by the guards. Chum had not been told what the alibi would be but, when questioned, Chum said they were trying to generate power for the hospital in case there was an operation at night. That was what Dr. Nance told them too. Whew!

Don did not get beriberi, but he was far too weak to walk anywhere to learn the news. And with no more radio broadcasts, current events were instead acted out high in the bright blue tropical sky, with American planes flying over.

From my diary:

2ⁿᵈ February, 1945. Rations further reduced to 10 ounces (rice and corn) per person. No meat to be supplied.

14th February, 1945. Notice for Monitors and for posting. Lieut. Kashmir, of the J. Garrison, has ordered that the camp be again reminded of the following rules and regulations:

No one is permitted to leave the area adjacent to his barracks after 7 p.m. except Wednesday and Sunday when the period is extended to 7:30 p.m. (All traffic, even crossing the roads between barracks, is forbidden.) <u>Hereafter anyone found disobeying this regulation is subject to being shot.</u>

I wrote down some trades for food that were made at this time.

Trades:

Mrs. Isla Corfield: her wedding ring (studded with small diamonds) for 4 kilos (2.2 lbs a kilo) of rice and 1 kilo brown sugar.

Mrs. Roy Wolfgram: a US$ 500 diamond ring for 13 kilos rice and 3 of brown sugar (she only got 2 of the sugar).

Mrs. Thomas: diamond earrings for 30 coconuts and 1 kilo rice.

Washington's Birthday, 22nd February, 1945. For the first time no food served on the chow line at all except a scoop of vegetables cooked in lots of water at 4:30 p.m. We were given a small Klim can full of palay (unhusked rice) *yesterday for today and tomorrow's rations. This afternoon the monitor announced there would be no more grain rations!! My golly, complete starvation. However, we are full of hope this evening as several P-38's came and dive-bombed pretty close to us. The poor internees have been working at their rice all yesterday and today to get a handful of rice to eat. When husked we get about 12 ounces for two days AND you have to provide your own firewood.*

The husk was completely inedible. Pound the grains and it was still there stuck to bits of rice. The consensus was to peel each grain. The whole camp was absorbed in dealing with this bit of madness.

Some of us had the strength to take what the Japanese offered for the first time. We could go outside under guard to pull weeds that we thought were edible. This was something my mother never taught me about, edible weeds?! I took a basket and followed the little Japanese guard. He led us up a steep slope and, with the sun burning down on the bedraggled group, we pulled lush green weeds by their roots (no knives allowed). Back at our cubicle, I cut off the roots for future use and with a smear of oil, sautéed stems and leaves and then covered the pan for several minutes, just before the bottom layer started to scorch. It certainly tasted good; besides, I had my fill and that was a most wondrous feeling. But not for long, as my stomach rebelled and kept me awake. I heard a distant rumble like tanks moving, but on a smooth surface. I told Ruth, my roommate, about the sound.

The next day, Friday, February 23, 1945, exploded like a magnificent fireworks display.

CHAPTER 22
RESCUE AND FREEDOM:
FEBRUARY 1945

From my diary:

Friday, 23rd February, 1945. There was constant plane activity last night. The pounding of guns sounded a little louder than usual. At 6 a.m. I had to make a trip to the adjacent building, and from then on I heard a continuous hum as if tanks were moving far away. Only it sounded too smooth for tanks or trucks.

6:20 a.m. Mr. Mora, our monitor, went through the corridor telling us the time. We have to be out on the road at 7 a.m., line up, bow to the little soldier and be counted. He is usually late.

7 a.m. Just as the gong sounded for roll call, nine planes droned slowly in front of the camp. They looked huge and black against the pale blue eastern sky. They were flying very low and I shouted to Ruth to come out NOW to see this miracle. The paratroopers dropped from the first plane, one by one, in rapid order. Nine planes emptied their human cargo until the air was filled with men dangling from parachutes.

I was so spellbound that I did not heed the gunfire that started inside our camp. Then, regaining my senses, I rushed back inside the barracks just in time to avoid a Japanese guard streaking down our hallway. Bullets whizzed past through the thin walls. One clipped a branch of a papaya tree a couple of yards way. Ruth and I sat on the floor and I was in the highest of spirits. Henry, who lived quite a ways down the road, rushed in and sat with us (he could have been killed.) "It's like firecrackers on Chinese New Year," I said.

I hurriedly lit my stove for the last time and used some of the coffee which we had saved two Christmases ago. Plus some sugar too, which cost 120 pesos a kilo two weeks ago, and good Filipino pesos too.

In no time at all the shooting stopped, and we ran outside and were greeted by big beautiful young men in strange dappled uniforms, arms outstretched to give us big hugs and to tell us, "YOU'RE FREE." Within minutes enormous tanks rolled along our main camp road. I was astonished to hear someone shouting, "Miss Lee, Miss Lee." It was a Captain Niemeyer, one of our rescuers, who wanted to interview Don and me.

Orders were given to evacuate our barracks at once. Some were told to take one suitcase while others did not have time even for that. In desperation, our rescuers torched the first of our "homes." With the sweeping wind, Barracks 3 & 4 (where the Japs lived) were burning, and soon one after another of these nipa buildings were on fire, making the camp a very hot spot. By 9 a.m. the last barracks were one big ball of fire.

Konichi and the commandant escaped, but most of the Japanese were killed in this raid. See Appendix II for a U.S. Army report on this famous rescue mission, in which all 2,146 internees were rescued with no civilian casualties.

W.H. Donald and Ansie being interviewed on Liberation Day
February 23, 1945

9 a.m. I was off on the amphibious tank No 3-5 with twenty-five other people: Don, A. D. Calhoun (Citibank), Ruth Swanson, missionary, Charles and Winnie Winn, Henry Sperry, Bob Cecil, C. C. Chapman and others. The sun was burning hot, and Ruth and I sat with our backs against a hole from which hot air rushed. In about half an hour, the tanks glided into the lake. It was hard to believe when told that these heavy metal boxes could float, but there we were chugging very slowly out to the middle of the lake. There was scary firing from the shore, and our gunner quickly aimed bullets in their direction. No one in the tank was hit. Empty 50 caliber shells rained on my back as I was directly beneath a gun. It was thrilling.

It was another couple of hours waiting on the beach on the other side. The sun could not have been much hotter. We drove for over an hour in a truck, passing cheering natives most of the way and arrived at the new Bilibid Prison in Muntinlupa.

Don was immediately driven back to Manila, where he stayed at the Philippine General Hospital and then moved to Santo Tomas. Later, I received a couple of notes from him, but did not see him again in Manila.

Henry was so sick that they immediately took him to the sick bay tent without my knowledge. I didn't find out where he was for several days.

Our first meal of the day, in fact our first meal under the American Flag, our first Freedom meal, was a small plateful of pea soup, and was it good! In the evening we were served tomato juice, corn beef stewed with diced carrots and peas, and asparagus. Far into the evening the chow line continued. People went several times.

In fact we were warned we could be harmed, or even die, from overeating. Going back in line was not as simple as it sounds. There were hundreds of us skeletons and we were outdoors under the scorching sun.

In the course of the evening I went for a quiet stroll. A young soldier joined me. He said, "It's great to be talking to a white woman again." I said, "Please look at me." He grinned and said, "You know what I mean." He was so homesick. I hope I was a help to him.

We are sleeping in large prison wards, double-deckers, hard boards but softened a little by army blankets. The first two nights hardly any of us slept at all as the Japs came from the mountains and attacked every night.

All through the night there was noise as our women and the young soldiers chatted in the hallway. I desperately needed sleep so I moved to an upper floor, leaving my friends behind.

26th February, 1945, Monday, 11:30 a.m. at Muntinlupa Prison. Planes are flying over this place dropping food by parachutes. They are beautiful—blue rayon ones. It really is a marvelous sight. The ex-internees are having a thrilling time. These cases are heavy and one dropped on top of our roof.

Ten days after liberation I weigh 103 lbs. Henry went back into the military field hospital, a large tent, in the Muntinlupa grounds on 3rd March. He collapsed while walking with me and another friend. He is in poor condition.

There were many frustrations in the field hospital. The one that sticks in my mind was that the Filipino aide would not give a patient a bedpan unless he was paid first.

In my diary I copied the following from the U.S. Army's *Free Philippines*:

> Manila, Monday, March 5, 1945
> Guerillas Hiked Two Days to Los Baños.
>
> Three hundred guerillas belonging to the Hunters, Hukbalahap and Marking units participated in the daring rescue of two thousand civilian internees in Los Baños prison camp on February 23.
>
> After a two day hike, the guerilla forces led by officers of the 11th Airborne Division surrounded the prison camp and waited for the signal to attack.
>
> Six internees who had previously escaped from the Los Baños camp joined the guerillas in the raid. Three Filipino guerillas without previous jump training bailed out with the Paratroopers.

It is with great sadness that I later read of a fearful retaliation by the Japanese after our rescue. Villagers in our camp's surrounding areas died at the hands of the Japanese in various horrible ways. Sadaki Konishi was tried for the offenses of violating the laws of war in six specifications. He ordered the murder of the following civilians: James Gardner, an American; his wife and infant son; and about fifty unnamed, non-combatant Filipino civilians and babies killed on March 5, 1945. He devised, aided and abetted in the gradual starvation of the Los Baños internees and the killing of George Louis, an American citizen. The trial lasted from November 23, 1945, to January 15, 1947. He was sentenced to "death by hanging."

The story of how we were plucked from certain death has been told in many publications. Most of us would not have survived much longer as the monitor of our barracks had announced that "there will be no more grain rations" just the day before our rescue. My admiration and gratitude to General Joseph M. Swing and those great soldiers who made the rescue possible are boundless. It was with the greatest of joy when, after Henry and I retired to California, General Swing and members of the 11th Airborne who took part in our rescue met at joint reunions with the internees and we all relived those bitter-sweet times in Los Baños.

CHAPTER 23
AFTER LIBERATION:
1945-1946

Don had been taken to hospital in Manila. Henry had disappeared into a makeshift hospital tent in the confines of the prison grounds. I was feeling like a lost soul. But not for long, as I was given two letters from home.

12th March, 1945. Received a telegram from Wing Sum [my fourth brother, J.S.] *from London. I am relieved that the family finally knows where I have been these last three and a half years.*

My third brother Harold wrote from Chungking:

> My dear Ansie,
>
> We were all so very, very glad to have your message telling us that you are safe and well. Everyone worried a lot about your safety until last year when I heard from George Greene that you were in Manila's Santo Tomas Camp. George Greene has just come out here and he called on me the other day and told me a lot about you and Donald.

I expect you will want to know what has happened to the family. Well, the great thing is everyone is still with us and no one suffered any physical harm in Hong Kong. Our home was bombed and subject to artillery fire after we had evacuated down to the Lee Theatre. I am afraid there's not much left of the house after the most terrific looting. We all gradually moved into Kweilin. I was the last to leave with Mother [Ah Ma, the first mother], Yee Chieh [Chieh, my own mother], Dione [our fifth sister] and Tat [our seventh brother] in August 1942. They all lived in Kweilin and I came up to Chungking by myself. Later, when I obtained a tiny little flat I moved Mother and Dione up in May 1943. Doris and Ken [her husband] had a house in Kweilin, and the youngsters [our younger siblings] were at school. Everything seemed alright until Kweilin was attacked and lost. Then Dick took charge of everyone and moved them up here. Unfortunately, Ken left everything too late and was cut off, so they have had to move down south. I am afraid Doris has had a terrible time. But I have located them by radio message, though we have had no letters.

We have found a nice place for Dick and his family, and Yee Chieh stays in my flat and sometimes with Dick. After a great deal of difficulty, the youngsters have managed to get into some sort of school. So you see we are carrying on all right although the burden is great…

I am making arrangements to remit you some funds – but getting foreign exchange here takes a little time. I hope to fix up something for you soon. I will remit to you c/o our consulate in San Francisco, so leave your address with the Chinese Consulate there. You know Deson & Marjorie Sze are in the New York office of the Bank of China.

Wing Sum *[our fourth brother J.S.]* has been in their London office for over a year and a half. He sees the Churchills often. You ought to write Mr. & Mrs. Churchill. Buster (their youngest son) is "missing" (I believe killed). Jack was a prisoner of war. Tom is a Brigadier General.

Mother has been in rather indifferent health for a long time. I hope the war will end soon and she can get back home. I hope you'll put on weight and get fit again. Keep me informed as to your plans and movements.

Love and kisses,

Harold

P.S. I hope you'll take the first opportunity to have a thorough physical check up. Take good care of yourself. This letter is coming to you through Deson Sze in N.Y.

P.P.S. I have wired Mr. K. P. Chen asking him to pay to you care of our Consulate San Francisco, US$2,000. Will you get the Chinese Consul to make out a certificate of your residence in U.S. as from the date of arrival as I require this immediately to obtain foreign exchange for you.

It could not have been a more heartwarming, loving letter.

Since Chieh was a truly devout Buddhist, I am sure that she must have prayed daily for me and that her prayers for my safety helped me through.

When the Japanese captured Hong Kong, there was not enough food to feed the inhabitants. Although South China was not as yet occupied by the Japanese, they allowed the Chinese in Hong Kong to cross the border to the mainland.

Almost everything from the family home was looted, not by the Japanese, but by the local people. They left only one thing of value: an enormous carved tusk. It was too big for a mere elephant, so it must have belonged to a mammoth. Father had bought it from the French Bank in Hong Kong. The carvings illustrated *The Story of the Three Kingdoms*, a historical novel. It now stands in the museum in the Chinese University, in Hong Kong.

Finally, on March 17, 1945, all of the Los Baños internees returned to Manila to stay again in the Santo Tomas compound.

The last entries in my camp diary:

17th March, 1945. Transferred from Muntinlupa to Santa Tomas.

23rd March, 1945. Henry came up for a visit. He has gained 18 lbs. Now 142 lbs. I am 105 lbs.

We all went through processing by officers (possibly medical) of some kind. They were just kids, and everything was lighthearted. It went like this, for me, anyway:

Army medical officer (very young): "How many children have you?"

Me: "I'm not married."

Officer: "What! Why don't you make hay while the sun shines?"

Me: "How do you know I'm not?"

He then glanced at my legs and said that I was all right. That ended the examination. I asked him for some vitamin B pills.

We waited our turn to board a ship to be repatriated to our homeland. However, Hong Kong was still under Japanese occupation. The war was far from over. So I was going to be "repatriated" to the United States, a country I had never set foot in before! (Although I had been to Honolulu in 1941, at that time Hawaii was not yet a state in the U.S.A.)

After a few weeks of anxious waiting, on April 9, 1945 I finally boarded a ship, the USS *Admiral Eberle, AP123.*

We sailed [from Manila] *on 10th April. Calm sea to Leyte. There were ten vessels with us. Waited at Leyte for over three days. It was awful waiting. Then suddenly, despite rumours, we set sail on Sunday with two destroyers only – leaving the other ships behind! I think Henry is on one of them. I was deathly seasick until we dropped anchor at the Carolinas. What an inspiring sight that was. A few wee islands and hundreds of ships of all kinds and sizes.*

The ship had been designed for carrying troops; there were over 3,000 women and children packed like sardines in the holds. There were hammocks slung below decks, but I never had to sleep in one. I was invited to share a cabin - a CABIN - with Mrs. Kuanson Young (no relation to the Young family I stayed with in Peking), widow of the Consul General from China who had been shot at the beginning of the Manila occupation. With her were her three daughters. The war was not over, and during nightfall there was a complete blackout above decks. It was stifling hot and 90 degrees in the cabin.

We stopped in Honolulu for only a few hours on April 27, 1945 (the band played for us), and on May 2, 1945 we finally made it to the United States.

2nd May, 1945. We docked at San Pedro. Weather chilly. Am wearing a WAC uniform with bright yellow socks! My silk stockings refuse to stay up.

Someone had given me a WAC uniform. It did not fit as I was still quite skinny. I was feeling very thankful to be on land again and what a land - the U.S.A.!

There was nothing to worry about as I was with Mrs. Young. She was taken to a hotel, and we were even given a suite when she said her accommodations were not large enough. It was sunny and cool. I received a sum of money from the British government and went to the biggest department store in Los Angeles and spent all the money on a light wool suit. At least when I went to San Francisco with Mrs. Young and her children, I would not look like a waif. I could not get any funds from home until I went to San Francisco.

In the meantime, Henry was still in the Philippines. When he landed in San Francisco on May 12, 1945, he went directly to the Palace Hotel to announce his arrival. The desk clerk had one look at him and said, "Sorry, no more rooms."

Henry told me later, "I was so used to being pushed around, I did not argue but sat in the lobby." (Of course there was a room reserved for him by the National City Bank of New York's corresponding bank in San Francisco.) Soon a group of Citibankers saw him, and he was escorted to share their beautiful suite. They were on their way to the Far East to re-open some of their branches.

While Henry sat despondently waiting in the lobby, couples and groups passed by. They were all dressed as if going to a ball. There were people of many nationalities. He did not know that here in San Francisco the signing of the United Nations Charter was taking place. The Palace Hotel was filled with diplomats and their entourages.

That same evening, Henry contacted me and we met at the cocktail lounge of my hotel. It was dimly lit, which was just as well, as they may not have admitted him looking like a scarecrow. His hair had been cut by a sailor from his ship who thought that putting a bowl on top of his head and snipping around it was a good idea and not a joke. His pants had been given to him by someone six inches shorter than he was. We were both so happy to be alive and together again. Our hearts filled with thankfulness and joy.

The next day was Sunday, and with the shops closed, Henry had no way to buy clothes. He went off to Oakland to visit distant relatives. When he boarded the bus and handed the fare to the bus driver, the latter refused the money, jumped out of his seat and addressed the passengers. "Please give this man a big hand—he has just come back from prison camp!" You can imagine how Henry must have felt.

Living in San Francisco was a happy and amazing time for me. I stayed with Mrs. Young and her three daughters. Henry introduced me to the Bank's chief lawyer from New York who was in San Francisco to observe the formation of the United Nations. The three of us had drinks at the Happy Valley Bar in the Palace Hotel twice. I think this meeting was fortuitous, because the bank lawyer had a chance to get to know me and so could vouch for me when the bank officials were later determining whether I was "suitable material" for one of their officers. In those days, Citibank officers posted abroad were not allowed to marry without the bank's permission—if you can imagine such an archaic practice!

The only Americans I knew were the Stilwells, from Peking days of 1936. "Doot" (Winifred) Stilwell Cox lived in Carmel, so my first relaxed time was a week there with her and her first child, Edward.

Ansie, Doot Stilwell Cox and baby Edward
Carmel, California 1945

I studied Mandarin at the University of California, Berkeley, where I lived at one of the fraternity houses. The International House, where I would have stayed, had been taken over by the army. My new friends howled at my British way of speaking. "Where are you going, Ansie?" they'd ask. "I'm going to take a tram to post a parcel," I'd say. "Oh no, you are not—you are going to take a trolley to mail a package." They were all dear girls and interested in my war years. When they learned that, no, I had not been raped, they were relieved and the questions tapered off.

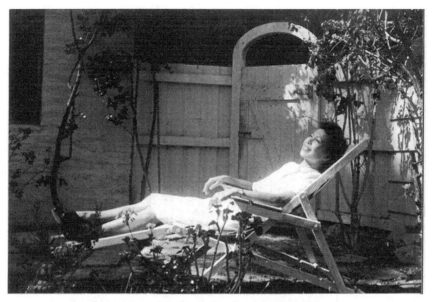

Peace at last, Carmel, California 1945

René Siu, Monsieur Ah-You's son from Tahiti, was also studying at Berkeley. So I had an old friend who took me to San Francisco to many shows and dinners. Tragically, René, his wife and three other Siu family members died in 1973 when their Pan Am plane crashed into the sea while leaving Tahiti.

I made life-long friends with the Nunans, parents of one of the students at Berkeley. They adopted me like one of their own and asked me to call them Mother Nunan and Dad Nunan. Any members of the Lee family who passed through San Francisco, usually on their way to college, stayed at the Nunans' home.

I was in San Francisco when the war with Japan finally ended.

14th August, 1945, 4:05 p.m., VJ Day. Official announcement of Japan's unconditional surrender. Bill [a friend I'd met at Berkeley] *took me down to Oakland and we found the streets jammed with sailors and the pavements ankle deep in paper. We ducked into side streets to avoid the drunken hordes.*

From San Francisco, I took a train to Chicago to visit Henry's Scandinavian cousins. I remember three charming ladies who came down from Muskegon to see who Henry was bringing into their lives. Their verdict: "She speaks better English than we do!" On to New York, where Henry met me and we took the Hudson Bay River Boat down to Manhattan.

Meeting my future mother-in-law should have been scary, but Mother Edith greeted me kindly. She lived in a house by the shore of the Atlantic Ocean, in Margate, New Jersey, just south of Atlantic City. She was Henry's stepmother, very straight-laced. She always dressed formally. (Perhaps that was normal in those days.) Even the butcher could not withstand her glare and gave her his best cuts. Mother Edith had a German housekeeper, who never failed to spoil us with delicious meals.

Ansie and Mrs. Henry M. Sperry, Sr.
Margate, New Jersey 1945

I lived at the International House in New York City for several months and took a course at Columbia University in creative writing, as well as a drawing class. The air during the winter was so sooty in the city that the windowsill of my small room at I-House was outlined with black. And my nose, when I returned home at the end of the day, was not much better. But New York City was wonderful, with a park down to the water's edge near Grant's Tomb close to where I stayed. We went by bus to the Cloisters in the north, by subway to the fish markets, and by ferry to the Statue of Liberty in the harbor.

One day Hollington Tong phoned me to say I should go see Madame H.H. Kung (Soong Ai-ling, Madame Chiang Kai-Shek's sister). I went to tea at her Waldorf Astoria apartment, but didn't stay very long.

When Henry returned to work at the head office of the First National City Bank of New York, he went to his boss and told him that he was planning to marry a Chinese girl. The brusque answer was: "Yes, I know." Someone in Washington had asked who Henry Sperry was! Washington? Henry returned to his desk, stunned. It turned out that my brother Harold had been invited to join the Chinese Ambassador to the Court of St. James, Quo Tai-Chi, when the latter came over from England to observe the big United Nations event in San Francisco. Perhaps it was the Ambassador himself? The bank was impressed.

Henry returned to Shanghai in January, 1946, but it was no simple matter for me to get space on a ship to China. It was not until June 1946 that I was allotted passage on a ship, the SS *M.C.*

Ansie & Henry in New York City, 1946

Meigs[22] in a cabin filled with women headed for Shanghai via Vancouver and Yokohama. I found out later that one of my cabin-mates was the future bride of my much admired "Chief," my boss in the Medical Relief Corps. What a stateroom! Can you picture

---

[22] Built as a troop transport ship, the former USS *General M.C. Meigs* was decommissioned in March, 1946 at San Francisco and transferred to the American President Lines as a passenger ship in the Pacific. She later carried troops in the Korean War. Source: "USS General Meigs (AP 116)," *Wikipedia.* Retrieved 12/1/08.

the space crammed with three tiered bunks, cheek by jowl? You can bet your life I was the only one not to wince at our situation. I was a jailbird, remember?

CHAPTER 24
SHANGHAI: 1946-1949

Wedding of Henry Muhlenburg Sperry and Ansie Lee

1ˢᵗ July, 1946. Docked at Pootung at 1:30 p.m. Henry looks wonderful. We got off the ship in fast time, sweat pouring off us– hot! Went to the Cheangs' house [sister Doris and her husband's family] *and had dinner.*

3ʳᵈ July, 1946. Am staying home all day as it is flooded outside. Chieh and Joyce [my fourth sister] *arrived at 5 p.m.*

I hadn't seen my mother in almost six years. It was wonderful to see her looking so well, after all she had been through during the war. The family had been split up because of the war, and she finally made it from Japanese-occupied Hong Kong to Chungking.

4ᵗʰ July, 1946. Agnes Greene [George Greene's wife] *took me to order flowers for the wedding. White gladiolas for me; purple ones for Joyce (yellow dress) and a pink-orange corsage for Chieh. Gardenias for Henry and Robbie* [the best man, Eddie Robertson] *and carnations for the ushers.*

Mr. K.P. Chen, Chairman and founder of the Shanghai Commercial Bank, gave me away, as eldest brother Dick was helping with rice allotments for the Hong Kong government.

On July 6, 1946, Mr. K. P. Chen stood at the entrance of the Church of England Holy Trinity Cathedral in Shanghai to escort me down the aisle to become the wife of Henry Muhlenburg Sperry. I wore a short white lace Chinese dress that I had made while waiting in San Francisco. I am no seamstress, but thought there would not be enough time to have it done in Shanghai. (Laughably, I could not have been more wrong because the expert seamstresses in Shanghai could make anything at short notice!) I had bought a pair of beautiful satin shoes at Joseph Magnin in San Francisco; the price was reduced when I asked!

The lovely home of the Manager of the National City Bank of New York was opened for our reception. There was a big gathering. When I was greeted with, "Happy the bride the rain fall upon," I replied in astonishment, "Oh, is it raining?" Raining! The Bank House garden where the reception was to be held had turned into a lake. I was running a low fever from a cold I had caught a few days ago. But I was oblivious of anything around me except how everyone was so very friendly and how happy I felt.

Henry M. Sperry and Ansie Lee's wedding
July 6, 1946

Don passes away

The same year, after a visit to Tahiti and ill with cancer, Don was flown by navy airplane to Oahu, Hawaii, then returned to Shanghai. My last visit with him was the night he passed away, November 9, 1946 at the Country Hospital in Shanghai. Madame Chiang knocked at his door to tell me to please leave and let him die. I felt so sad not to be able to give him any comfort if he wanted me to stay. Earlier in the day, Don had given Henry all his precious papers and told him to burn them. Henry was late for dinner that evening; he was down in the basement filling up the furnace with Don's precious papers.

"Did you see anything?" I asked. "Only what was on top of the pile," Henry answered. It was the decoration Don had received from the Japanese.[23]

If anyone wonders what happened to Don's memoirs that everyone thought he wrote, he never wrote one word. Some of the tales would have destroyed confidences, and Don did not want to do that to his friends. He told people that all his papers had been destroyed during the war, and now he was making sure that none would exist after he died.

Don was buried the next day, the first foreigner to be buried in Shanghai's Hungjao cemetery. Henry was one of the pallbearers.

---

[23] In 1908 Donald had received a minor Japanese decoration for his coverage of the Russo-Japanese War (1904-05). *Australian Dictionary of Biography Online Edition.* Retrieved 1/1/09.

Don inscribed this photo, taken in Honolulu in 1941,
to Ansie shortly before he died.

Life in Shanghai

Living in Shanghai was the best of all worlds. The bank's Head Office gave approval for us to have a home that Henry had found, on Rue Cohen in the French Concession. It was a two-story building with a large living and a dining room, and suited us.

All of our parties were given at home. With our excellent cook, Chong, who had worked for Henry before the war, his wife, and a young man who always finished whatever he was doing (even though you asked him for immediate help on something else), we never needed to call in caterers for our entertaining. One thing was important: we needed a driver. To get in trouble with the law was not worth the hassle. If you have a car you have to employ a driver, said the Head Office.

My dear childhood amah, Ah Cow, with her daughter, came up from Hong Kong to cook Chinese food, to sew, and to be my personal maid. Her daughter, whom we tried to educate, became our "pet amah," in charge of the dachshund and cat that were great pals and slept in the same large wicker basket. They entertained our guests with hide and seek behind the drapes when we had a party. They never did it any other time!

We enjoyed playing tennis at the French Club near our home on Avenue Gascogne in the French Concession. My experience playing against my brothers' friends at home in Hong Kong came in handy.

Ansie with dachshund pups at 3 weeks old

We stayed in Shanghai until 1949 when the communists were about to take over the city. That was when the currency went crazy. When Henry left for work in the morning he would ask me how much money I needed for that day. If I had to do some shopping, I would say $100,000? He would counter with, "Here's $500,000." The brand new notes were printed in the U.S. Each hour brought higher prices. Henry said it was much worse than the inflation in Germany after WWI. Bob Strong, our very good friend who worked for the U.S. Banknote Co., was kept busy ordering supplies from the U.S. One of Henry's favorite pictures was of himself sitting on a crate of banknotes on the Shanghai wharf, titled, "Assets over a Million."

Ansie and Henry at the French Club, Shanghai 1946

Towards the end of 1949, we left Shanghai. The communists came in soon after. One of our bank officers stayed, and it was only after lengthy negotiations for a large sum of money that he was allowed to leave.

In Hong Kong, Henry continued to work for the bank. My large and loving family had all returned from their travails of war, unharmed. I bore a son, Frederick Muhlenburg, and a daughter Victoria, named after Hong Kong's capital. How lucky they were to grow up in Hong Kong, surrounded by loving grandmothers and aunts and uncles galore and built-in playmates of so many cousins. When Hank (as everyone other than family called him) was in charge of the bank in Hong Kong, we met many interesting people, sometimes through the U.S. Consul-General; His Excellency, the Governor; my brothers; and, of course, our own Citibank. It was an exciting life.

So started many long years of another adventure—this time not quite so outrageous, but certainly not dull. Now living in the Bay Area, south of San Francisco, at a retirement home in Portola Valley, I am surrounded by an aura of friendship, caring, and love. As always God protects me with his great patience and loving kindness. Thank you, Lord.

Fred, Vicky, Ansie and Henry
Hong Kong 1966

Henry and Ansie at the Summer Palace
Beijing 1980

Appendix I   LEE FAMILY TREE

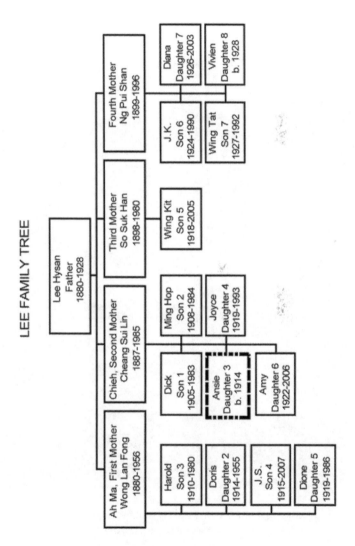

LEE FAMILY TREE

Lee Hysan
Father
1880-1928

Ah Ma, First Mother
Wong Lan Fong
1880-1956

Chieh, Second Mother
Cheang Sui Lin
1887-1985

Third Mother
So Suk Han
1898-1980

Fourth Mother
Ng Pui Shan
1899-1996

Harold
Son 3
1910-1980

Doris
Daughter 2
1914-1955

J.S.
Son 4
1915-2007

Dione
Daughter 5
1919-1986

Dick
Son 1
1905-1983

Ansie
Daughter 3
b. 1914

Amy
Daughter 6
1922-2006

Ming Hop
Son 2
1908-1984

Joyce
Daughter 4
1919-1993

Wing Kit
Son 5
1918-2005

J.K.
Son 6
1924-1990

Wing Tat
Son 7
1927-1992

Diana
Daughter 7
1926-2003

Vivien
Daughter 8
b. 1928

From left: Ansie with sisters Joyce, Dione and Amy
Hong Kong, 1966

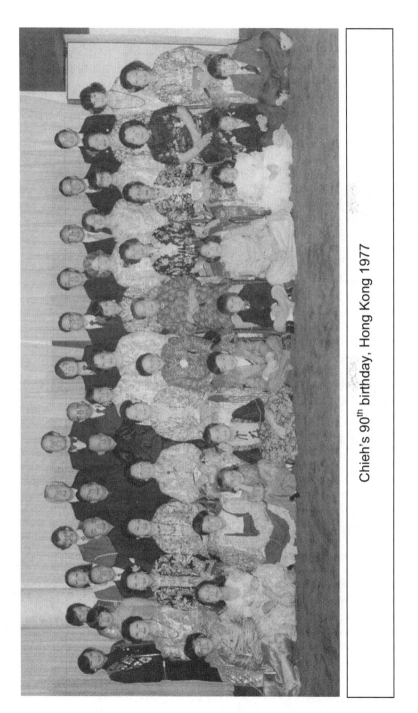

Chieh's 90th birthday, Hong Kong 1977

The seven Lee Brothers
Hong Kong, c. 1960

APPENDIX II

REPORT FROM
U.S. ARMY XIV CORPS
ON THE RELEASE
OF LOS BAÑOS INTERNEES

About two weeks after our liberation Henry gave me a carbon copy of a report typed on thin foolscap. It is now yellow and friable after more than sixty years in my rattan picnic basket. I have taken excerpts from it.

A REPORT FROM U.S. ARMY XIV CORPS ON THE RELEASE OF LOS BAÑOS INTERNEES

Realizing the extreme brutality of the enemy, which experience had shown reached new depths with the proximity of liberating troops, GHQ decided on the 4th of February, to rescue these unfortunate Americans and Allies.

The Sixth Army vested the mission of the rescue to the XIV Corps, who for this purpose had been assigned the 11th Airborne Division. Field Order No. 18, dated February 21, 1945 stated "The LOS BAÑOS Force will move to LOS BAÑOS by airborne, motor, amphibious, and foot, and will relieve the LOS BAÑOS internees and return them to MUNTINLUPA Hospital."

Regardless of what plan was developed for the rescue, it was quite obvious that a very detailed study of the prison site, together with the approaches thereto, would have to be made. It was, therefore, decided to infiltrate selected personnel into the area to study the possibility of a parachute drop, suitability of the landing beach for an amphibious operation, and routes of approach for land troops. Major Vanderpool, GHQ representative with the guerrillas in BATANGAS PROVINCE, was contracted, and a plan of the camp prepared with the help of his associates, escaped internees, and civilians living in the vicinity. This map was so detailed as to include the location of barracks and other buildings, particularly those containing weapons and ammunition, together with the designation of covered approach routes for small groups detailed to surprise and kill the sentinels.

… It was planned that the LOS BAÑOS Force would move on 23 February at 0700 to rescue the internees and transport them to an area behind our lines where they could receive medical attention and food. This hour was chosen because it was known that the enemy would be engaged in calisthenic drills at the time and a minimum number armed. It was believed that it would be less hazardous for the internees to be moved across waters of LAGUNA DE BAY to MAMATID…. From MAMATID they were to be transported by motor vehicle to the NEW BILIBID PRISON at MUNTINLUPA, where succor could be given.

… It was necessary that an infiltrating force should be just outside the gates of the internment camp at the time when parachute troopers dropped and the water-borne infantry arrived. The Division Reconnaissance Platoon, accompanied by two escaped internees and an especially selected guerilla group was designated as this force. This Platoon embarked 36 hours prior to H-hour in native bancas, landing near the site of LOS BAÑOS... Part of the Platoon secured the drop zone and signaled to the airborne infantry by columns of white phosphorous smoke. Another group secured the beachhead and signaled the amphibious force by two smoke columns. The third group had succeeded in getting to within 15 yards of the guards at the main gate by moving up the deep ravine shown on Sketch No. 36. As the first parachute opened, this group opened fire on the enemy, so effectively that there was only a little mopping up to be done when Company B of the 511th Parachute infantry arrived.

At 0515, the amphibious force … embarked on 54 amphibian tractors ... entered the water at MAMATID.... It is a tribute to the navigation skill of the Commanding Officer of the Amphibian Tractor Battalion that he was able to direct the column through pitch black darkness entirely by compass, over an unfamiliar course and to land his troops at one minute before scheduled H-hour.

Nine C-47's took off from NICHOLS FIELD at 0630 with Company B of the 511th Parachute Infantry aboard. At 0658, two columns of white phosphorous smoke arose from the drop zone telling the paratroopers that the Division Reconnaissance Platoon had accomplished its first mission. Green lights blinked in the ships and jumpers left the planes. All men landed in the drop zone without injury, in a perfect pattern, assembled in three minutes, and arrived at the camp 17 minutes after the first parachute opened. Enroute to the camp, this Company reduced one pill box containing a light machine gun. Upon arrival they killed the few remaining Japanese, set up a perimeter defense around the camp, and began to organize the internees for evacuation.

… Thus ended the rescue of the LOS BAÑOS internees, an operation brilliantly conceived and meticulously executed, in which 2146 American citizens and Allied subjects were liberated from the Japanese and brought to safety.

56718593R00158

Made in the USA
Lexington, KY
28 October 2016